Revised Edition

The High Performance Bank

Insights and Advice on How to Make Your Bank a Consistent Top Performer

Albert J. Brown, Jr.

A BANKLINE PUBLICATION
PROBUS PUBLISHING COMPANY
Chicago, Illinois
Cambridge, England

BANKLINE

A BankLine Publication

CONTENTS

PREFACE

This book is written to help directors and managers of community banks in the United States that are located outside major money center cities. Much of what is written about banking today comes from experts in financial centers. The financial instruments and strategies they describe may work well in the 50 largest banks in the nation; however, major banks fund their earning assets differently than banks in Iowa and Vermont, and money center banks loan to a different segment of the market. Community banks that try to compete in major cities must adopt different strategies to succeed. Additionally, banks that depend on core deposits to fund their assets should employ different approaches than those that concentrate more on purchased money.

As a bank consultant, I regularly meet with the senior management groups of community banks. We present a day-long workshop designed to improve earnings in their specific bank. We try to have as many officers present as possible so everyone in the bank understands what is being done and why it is being done. This helps to produce widespread support for the strategies to be employed. We highlight the areas in which that particular bank has the best opportunities for improvement, and then we present a list of possible strategies by which that improvement might be accomplished.

The contents of this book are based on actual experience. Improved earnings did not happen by coincidence or accident. General principles and guidelines were explained, then management was left to apply those principles and guidelines in its own bank. The strategies worked for them, and they can work for you. We simply concentrated the management groups' efforts in certain critical areas, and then existing management produced superior earnings. In these pages, we do not emphasize classroom theory—we present strategies followed by real bankers, which have worked in real banks.

This book is the result of several consultations that generally take about one full day. On several occasions, I have been asked for a written transcript of my presentation. This book grew out of those requests.

The path to superior earnings is easy to understand; it doesn't involve any complicated math or esoteric theories. Unfortunately, it is not easy to accomplish. Each step of the way involves simple principles whose successful execution never allows us to follow the path of least resistance. That shouldn't surprise anyone; if it were easy, all banks would produce great earnings. We must realize that if we do what all the other banks are doing, we will be average.

I want somehow to recognize all those people who have contributed to the data file in my brain. I have been president of a mortgage company and president and chairman of a commercial bank and chairman of a distressed real estate company. In those capacities I've been helped by dozens of very competent professional bankers. I have learned something from almost everyone I have ever known. I have read articles by dozens of people, listened to lectures by countless others, and read many books over the past 30 plus years. While all of these have influenced me in some way, I think those with whom I most closely agree are Paul Nadler and Tom Peters. I do not pretend to possess their level of professionalism or to share their management knowledge and expertise. I have listened to both of them speak, and I'm sure their talks and writings are intricately commingled within my head, along with ideas and conclusions which I have worked out by trial and error over the years.

I have heard Paul Nadler at Stonier (and on several other occasions) and he always seemed to have a common-sense answer to what are considered by most to be very complicated problems. Too many people are reluctant to accept simple answers. They seem to think that if the solution doesn't require an MBA and a computer, it won't work.

Finally, I would like to recognize the contribution to my banking education made by Victor J. Riley, Jr., CEO of Key-Corp, and all of the Corporate Staff members. I would also like to acknowledge the help of our original Asset Liability Committee, as well as the new members who have joined that group over the years. While the people mentioned have added in some way to my banking education, none of us agree on everything, so I don't want to suggest that all of my views are supported by them.

I feel an obligation to give credit for every thought expressed in this book, but after more than 30 years in banking I can no longer remember which ideas originated in my brain, which came from someone else, and which were a combination of the two. I hope it is sufficient to thank all of you with whom I've worked and from whom I've learned, and to thank all the teachers, lecturers, and writers who have contributed in some way to what currently resides within my mind and on these pages.

Although the ideas discussed throughout this work are aimed at senior management, in some chapters I will define certain standard banking terms. This is done because I realize some readers will not have the experience of a senior level banker, and I want to be sure that I'm making myself clear. I apologize in advance to those who don't need the definitions.

1 GOAL SETTING

In theory at least, banking is a very simple business. Banks take in deposits and lend them out. If banks don't make loans, they don't make money, and if banks don't have deposits, they can't make loans. The whole process starts with a deposit. We can't increase the size of the bank by making loans. Our bank can only grow by increasing deposits or borrowing money.

Before trying to formulate policies, plans, or strategies, we should briefly consider exactly what banks do. Why are there banks at all? What is their reason for being? What purpose do they serve? We might mistakenly believe the primary goal of the bank is to make money. If we start out with that assumption, we might then logically conclude that banks should be involved in any enterprise that can be profitable. This is not the case.

A BANK'S BASIC FUNCTIONS

Banks perform two or three basic functions for society, and we should agree on those functions if we expect to agree on anything else. Banks provide people with a safe place to store their money, and banks sometimes pay interest on

that money while it's being stored. Banks also make it easy
for people to transfer money in an extraordinarily inexpen-
sive and efficient manner in order to make payments. Finally, banks lend money to individuals, businesses, and
governmental units, and in the process banks increase the
nation's money supply making economic growth possible.
The net result of all of this is that banks take money from
people who have more than they need at the moment and
make it available to people who have less than they need at
the moment. In short, banks make sure that the collective
wealth of a community is put to efficient use in a safe way.
If we can focus on these things as the reason that banks
exist, then we can build our plans. Otherwise, we won't be
sure what goals to establish, or be able to tell if we're even
moving in the right direction. This doesn't mean banks
should not provide any other services. It merely means that
if banks don't do those basic things for which they were
originally designed, then we could find ourselves providing corollary services in a very professional way and simultaneously find ourselves out of the banking business. The
purpose of this book is to explain how to produce high
earnings in the banking business, not in any other business.

Some bankers today seem to believe that in order to produce good bank earnings, they must become involved in
other businesses. We do not subscribe to this belief. If we
know more about banking than any other business, and we
can not produce satisfactory earnings in banking, how can
we hope to excel at anything else?

Other firms can sell insurance or securities and provide
data processing or tax preparation services. Banks may also
provide these services and do so profitably. In fact, a valid
case may be made for allowing banks to provide these
services, if in so doing they don't hurt the bank's ability to
perform those activities for which banks were originally
founded.

WHEN BANKS FAIL AT BASIC FUNCTIONS

When banks fail to perform their basic functions perfectly, other businesses have an opportunity to move in and take over a part of the bank's activities. When banks couldn't pay market rates on deposits (because of government regulation), brokerage firms developed and introduced money market accounts. Long before the banking industry offered charge cards on a widespread basis, retail stores offered their own, thereby entering the lending business. Savings institutions developed NOW accounts so they could offer demand deposits. More and more companies are borrowing in the commercial paper market thereby bypassing the banking industry by going directly to the depositor. Hundreds of Wall Street firms offer mutual funds thereby drawing savings deposits out of banks. Automobile manufacturers offer car loans and leases. Other manufacturers develop companies to finance their own products. Dozens of different kinds of businesses lend money through various means, but that doesn't mean they are banks. It also doesn't mean banks should be in the same businesses as Sears or General Motors simply because those companies are encroaching on the banking industry's turf.

While a good case can be made for allowing banks to provide a wide array of services for a fee, it is more difficult to accept the notion that banks should be able to invest their depositors' money in other businesses. The bank has an obligation to safeguard the depositors' funds. It is one thing to risk the shareholders' money in nonbanking activities. It is another thing entirely to risk the depositors' money in nonbanking activities. Depositors are merely lending their money to the bank. This transaction is not the same as supplying a business with risk capital. Depositors have a right to expect bankers to cautiously manage their money. Making properly underwritten loans to creditworthy borrowers does not entail the same degree of risk as taking an ownership position in a shopping mall or computer services company. New businesses have a failure rate that is dozens of times higher than the charge-off rate on loans. If banks fail at an inordinately high rate, they will no longer be perceived as a safe place to keep funds and they will forfeit one of their reasons for being. Without deposits, there is no bank. If banks are no safer than insurance companies or stock brokerage firms, the public will eventually abandon banks and use those other businesses for services that have traditionally belonged to banks alone. This is happening right now.

So where is all this leading? We believe it is imperative that we focus our attention on the primary functions of banks. It is critical to high performance banking that we determine how to become high performing banks, not high performing insurance companies. High performing banks should out earn their peers year after year. Not just for the year or two in which they got lucky, and not just for the year or two when the "hot button" worked.

Recent banking history is full of shooting stars that momentarily outshone all others and then were gone. High performing banks may never come in first, but their earnings will be in the top 10% year after year.

BEING A CONSISTENT HIGH PERFORMER

To be a repeat high performer, a bank must recognize the risk levels that are consistent within the industry and not accept higher risks to produce temporarily higher profits. Higher than normal risk eventually produces higher than normal losses. Banks should not attempt to produce above average earnings by accepting above average risks. Because banks are so thinly capitalized, they can never afford to have a really bad year. Two such years in a row can put many banks out of business.

There is certainly an element of risk involved in banking, as there is in any business. Although it is often tempting, bankers should not accept just any kind of risk that holds promise of a greater reward. The larger the risk, the greater the reward, but also the higher the probability of failure. When banks fail too frequently, they forfeit their claim to safety. Banks that are perceived to be unsafe must pay more for their money which usually only worsens their earnings problems.

Stick to the Basics

Consistently high performing banks must stick to the basics. They must confine their activities to providing a safe place for the public's excess funds and to making prudent loans so the collective wealth of a community can be put to good use. They may also supply any number of other services for a fee, but they should not accept inordinate risk by taking an ownership position in other businesses. Ownership positions in data processing, life insurance, discount brokerage, or any other financial subsidiary should be undertaken through a holding company, together with proper separation safeguards which protect the soundness of the bank.

The first rule of high performance banking is to confine risk-taking to the business of banking. Bankers who wish to engage in venture capital type investments should not use depositor's money. To produce consistently higher-than-average earnings, we should stick to the basics.

It is unclear why, but many people tend to take unnecessary risks. Perhaps it is understandable in the case of a trapeze artist. Such people get paid for taking extraordinary risks, and they must feel an emotional high. But why should anyone accept an unnecessary risk in the business world when there is no commensurate reward? Why loan money to the local automobile dealer at the same rate of interest that is available on a government bond?

There is also a reluctance in human nature to leave well enough alone. Many times banks produce high returns on equity several years in a row and it's as if they get bored; they have to change direction. Imagine Coca-Cola changing their formula every two or three years. While we should continually strive to improve service, we shouldn't make major changes in strategy in a high performing bank. A certain constancy of purpose and direction is necessary. There is room in banking for thinkers and innovators. In fact, there is a crying need for them, but we shouldn't abandon proven strategies while they are still working. We can't patent ideas and banking runs on ideas. Any service we introduce will be immediately copied if it's any good.

Drastic change may be required to change a mediocre bank into a high performing bank. But once that bank is humming, in order to maintain consistent high performance year after year, future change should be gradual and focused on the long haul. We can't expect to tear down systems and philosophies and replace them with new ones without producing disruptions in steady earnings streams. If we have a poorly performing bank, many changes may be required and temporary disruptions may need to be tolerated until everything is moving on the right track. But once we have a high performing bank, additional changes should be undertaken judiciously.

Resistance to Change

Before we give the idea that we're opposed to change, we'd better explain further because nothing could be further from the truth. Most people will accept the notion that for conditions to improve, change must take place. We would all like to see things improve at work, at home, and in the world generally. We all must recognize that change is necessary. Why then do most of us resist change so strenuously? We accept the **need for** change in the entire world, but not at ground zero. We know that we are not perfect, so why can't we change? Why is it so hard to give up old concepts and beliefs and adopt new ones? Perhaps because change always produces stress. Nonetheless, we must recognize that resistance to change is the single largest impediment to moving an average bank into the ranks of the high performers.

Commitment to Change

To change an average performing bank into a high performer, every officer in that bank—starting with the president—must make a firm, that is a FIRM, commitment to reevaluate current beliefs and policies in the light of new evidence. For this to work, everyone must change at least a little. We're not talking light lip service here. We all must promise, pledge, and swear that we will give each idea a new look from all sides. We must open our minds and not resist every new idea.

We don't accept the notion that we can't teach an old dog new tricks. There are elderly people who constantly search for new ideas, concepts, and philosophies. They are eagerly learning new things every day of their lives. There are others of the same age who haven't had a new idea in 40 years. On the other hand, there is nothing sadder than a 30-year-old bank officer who can't accept new ideas because he's already learned all he's ever going to.

A somewhat less obvious objection to change occurs when the banker says, "Maybe that's a good idea and maybe it worked in other places, but it won't work here. Our customers are different." Sure they are. Now we have to prove that the people in Albany, New York, are the same as the people in Albany, Oregon. We all know they are not identical; but in basic needs and values, they are close enough. The man who runs a McDonald's in Albany, Oregon, needs the same bank services as the man who runs a McDonald's in Albany, New York. The gas station operator in Portland, Oregon, needs the same bank services as the person who runs a gas station in Portland, Maine. What works in Portland, Maine, works in Portland, Oregon. It also works just about every place else. Location is not a valid excuse for resisting change.

How many of these other change resisting, new idea killers have you heard?

- "We tried that once and it didn't work." Maybe we didn't do it right the last time, let's try it again.

- "Our customers are different." So are snowflakes but plows still get the job done.

- "If we did that the regulators wouldn't like it." The regulators are constantly changing and what they liked last year they may dislike this year. If we always follow the advice of bank regulators and our bank fails, guess who loses his job?

- "Our employees couldn't do that." Well maybe they couldn't so it's up to us to train them. In a constantly changing world, constantly training employees is a necessity, not an option.

- "You have to be practical and that's not practical."

- Along with, "That's not logical." If we are dealing with a flawed or incomplete knowledge base, a lot of logical things can seem illogical.

- "If we did that, we'd lose all our customers." Fortunately for most bankers, there is virtually nothing we can do that will drive away all of our customers.

- "It's not in the budget." So what! Nothing new is ever in the budget. Somebody in the bank must be smart enough to know that blindly worshiping the "budget" is seldom the wisest thing to do.

- "Why change? Things are working the way they are." This is closely akin to the terrible, "If it's not broke, don't fix it." American industry has been saying this for about 25 years now. It even seems to make sense; sounds like irrefutable homespun wisdom. It's another way of saying, "Leave well enough alone." In the meantime, the Japanese have been saying, "If it's not perfect, make it better."

While Detroit was practicing the, "If it's not broke, don't fix it" philosophy, the Japanese were making cars better and better and better and better. By the time Detroit woke up, it was much too late.

Banking laws, regulations, technology, products, pricing, and service quality are changing every single day. Today's high quality service will be considered average in three years and unsatisfactory in five. The world of banking will change even if we don't. The only choice we really have is whether or not we will be left behind.

While we recognize that not all change is for the better, we must also accept that for things to get better, there must be change and it must start with us. We cannot change the world, but we can change this little piece of it that we inhabit and influence. A bank-wide commitment to actively pursue change is necessary.

LITTLE THINGS MEAN A LOT

The difference between mediocre and outstanding performance in banking equals about one-half of one percent of total assets. Someone once said that there is very little difference among men but what little difference there is, is of extreme importance.

Looking to the world of sports may supply a satisfactory analogy. If a baseball player gets five hits out of every 20 at bats, his batting average is .250 and he is average. If he gets six hits out of every 20 at bats, his batting average is .300 and he is a superstar. He is rewarded with multiyear multimillion dollar contracts. The difference between mediocre and outstanding is one base hit in every 20 at bats.

Take a quick look at the next chart.

National League—1991

		W-L	Runs/ Game	Hit/ Game	ERA
Best Record	Pittsburgh	98–64	4.74	8.85	3.44
Worst Record	Houston	65–97	3.73	8.30	4.00

The difference in runs scored per game between the teams with the best and worst records in the league was a single run. The difference in hits per game was a little over one hit per two games. The difference in earned run average of their respective pitching staffs was similar. Lest we think 1991 was an unusual year, let's check out 1992.

National League—1992

		W-L	Runs/ Game	Hit/ Game	ERA
Best Record	Atlanta	98–64	4.21	8.59	3.14
Worst Record	Los Angeles	63–99	3.38	8.23	3.41

The differences between the best and worst in 1992 were even less than those records in 1991. It's like that in banks as well. Banks are so highly leveraged that small changes can produce material differences in the bottom line. Very often, the only difference between average and outstanding bank performance is that the outstanding bank does 100 little things slightly better than the average bank.

EARNINGS GOALS FOR A HIGH PERFORMANCE BANK

For any nonbankers who may be reading this, the earning/asset ratio is the most common measure of bank performance. Dividing net after-tax income by total assets produces this ratio. A $100-million-dollar bank that earns one million dollars would have an earning/asset ratio of 1.00%. High performing banks have earning/asset ratios over 1.00%. It is easier to accomplish for smaller banks with fewer layers of management, but even large banks can exceed this ratio. Sometimes the earning/asset ratio is called the return on assets. They are the same thing.

This ratio tells us how well we're doing with the assets at our disposal. It measures how well we're doing with what we have—total assets. Others feel return on equity is a more important gauge of performance because it measures how well we're doing for our stockholders. Return on equity is simply net income divided by total equity. Total equity is what is left in the bank after all assets have been converted into cash and all debts and all depositors have been paid in full. It is what the bank is worth after everything has been liquidated.

We feel comfortable establishing earnings goals expressed as a return on assets or a return on equity. However, these two measurements can sometimes conflict with each other. Consider the following.

Total Equity = Total Assets × Equity Ratio
Net Income = Return on Assets × Total Assets
Net Income = Return on Equity × Total Equity

Things equal to the same thing are equal to each other; therefore:

ROA × Total Assets = ROE × Total Equity

And if we substitute in the above formula for Total Equity we get:

ROA × Total Assets = ROE × Total Assets × Equity Ratio

Divide both sides by Total Assets and the end result is:

ROA = ROE × Equity Ratio

For those who couldn't follow all of the algebra, take our word for it, return on assets equals return on equity x the equity ratio.

That means, if the equity ratio doesn't change, then the only way to increase return on equity is to increase return on assets, and vice versa. However, it also means that if we reduce the equity ratio and return on assets stays the same, then the return on equity must increase. The way to reduce the equity ratio is to increase the size of the bank either through new deposits or borrowed funds.

Perhaps a glance at Table 1.1 more clearly demonstrates what we're talking about. As we can see, with an equity ratio of 8%, in order to produce a return on equity of 15%, we need a return on assets of 1.20%. If the equity ratio is 7.5%, then it only requires an ROA of 1.13% to produce a 15% ROE. And if we have an equity ratio of 6.0%, we only need a return on assets of .90% to achieve an ROE of 15%.

The amount of profits a bank can produce is more a factor of its total size than its equity. Consider two banks, the first with $100 million in assets, $8 million in equity and

Table 1.1   **Return on Assets Required**

Capital Ratio	Return on Equity					
	13.00%	**14.00%**	**15.00%**	**16.00%**	**17.00%**	**18.00%**
8.00%	1.04	1.12	1.20	1.28	1.36	1.44
7.50%	0.98	1.05	1.13	1.20	1.28	1.35
7.00%	0.91	0.98	1.05	1.12	1.19	1.26
6.50%	0.85	0.91	0.98	1.04	1.11	1.17
6.00%	0.78	0.84	0.90	0.96	1.02	1.08
5.50%	0.72	0.77	0.83	0.89	0.94	1.01

an equity ratio of 8%. The second bank has total assets of $133.3 million, $8 million in equity and an equity ratio of 6%. Both have the same amount of equity, but one has total assets of $100 million and the other $133.3 million. Which one will make more money and produce a higher return on equity? All things being equal, bet on the bigger bank. Because experienced bankers understand this, if earnings goals and bonus plans are measured by a return on equity, there is a tendency to leverage the bank by borrowing money or paying higher rates for certain deposits. This allows the bank to obtain more investable funds. The net result of this activity is usually a lower equity ratio, a lower return on assets, and a higher return on equity. Some checks and balances need to be established so the bank won't go too far in this direction thereby accepting a lower equity ratio than the board might deem acceptable.

Profit goals should not be established until a minimum equity ratio is agreed upon by the board. Otherwise, there is the above mentioned tendency to increase the size of the bank by buying expensive money and reinvesting at very small spreads. This reduces the equity ratio and increases income slightly. At some point the question of the bank's safety must be considered. A bank with a low loan/deposit ratio or a bank with extremely low delinquent and classified loans might feel comfortable with a smaller capital ratio. The more problem loans we have, the more capital we'll need to fall back on if those loans eventually prove to be uncollectible. The board should determine what level of capital is satisfactory, and management should stay within the board's guidelines.

Once we, our board, and anyone else who has input decides on a minimum equity ratio, then it doesn't matter if we set performance goals in terms of return on equity or return on assets. We can't improve one without improving the other. If, as some banks do, we publicly announce our performance goals, they should be mathematically consistent. If our bank has an equity ratio of 8.0%, we can't have earnings goals of 15% ROE and 1.0% ROA. They're not mathematically compatible. With an equity ratio of 8.0% an ROA of 1.0% produces an ROE of 12.5%. We have to increase our ROA goals, reduce our ROE goals, or reduce our equity ratio.

Regardless of our capital ratio, we should produce a return on equity of at least 15%, and to be a really top performer, 16% to 18%. After we've settled on an ROE goal and an equity ratio, then we'd pick the ROA that gives the desired results and that's our target.

Let's start with a 6.5% capital ratio, a return on assets of 1.0% and a return on equity of 15% as our goals. (We know, we're off two basis points; we rounded.) If we want an ROE of 16%, we'll have to raise our ROA goal to 1.05%. That's also fine. If our bank is currently well below these levels, we should probably start with a lower goal, at least for the short term. Officer bonus plans that run off earnings should kick in at 15% ROE and work up quickly from there. Officers shouldn't be paid bonuses for producing average results.

GROWTH GOALS

Once we've settled on earnings goals, we should think about growth goals. Again, they must be consistent. If we don't change our equity ratio, then our bank can't grow any faster than our equity grows. The amount our equity grows depends on two things, earnings and the divided payout ratio. If we have a return on equity of 15% and we pay out one-third of that (5%) in dividends, there's 10% left. That means our equity has grown 10% and our bank can grow 10%. The more we pay out in dividends, the less earnings we retain, and the less we can grow.

Table 1.2 shows the annual growth rate possible with various returns on equity versus various dividend payout ratios. If our bank has an ROE of 16% and it pays out half of its earnings in dividends, it can only grow 8% per year. If it only pays out 25% of the 16%, it can grow 12% a year. A board of directors that wants a high growth rate must understand that it is mathematically impossible without a low dividend payout.

Again, we can set whatever goals we want, but we must be sure they are mathematically consistent. We can't pay

Table 1.2   Annual Growth Rate Possible

Dividend Payout Ratio	Return on Equity			
	10%	12%	14%	16%
20%	8.0%	9.6%	11.2%	12.8%
25%	7.5%	9.0%	10.5%	12.0%
30%	7.0%	8.4%	9.8%	11.2%
35%	6.5%	7.8%	9.1%	10.4%
40%	6.0%	7.2%	8.4%	9.6%
45%	5.5%	6.6%	7.7%	8.8%
50%	5.0%	6.0%	7.0%	8.0%

out half our earnings in dividends and have growth in assets and earnings of 10% unless our return on equity exceeds 20%. The arithmetic doesn't allow it. Our board must decide whether it wants big dividends or big growth. We would choose big growth because, if our bank is ever sold, the purchaser will pay a premium on our book value, not on our previous dividends. Even if our bank isn't sold, our stock will sell as a percentage of book value (hopefully, over 100% of book) or as a multiple of earnings, and we won't earn a premium on past dividends.

If we are already paying out more than we'd like, it's probably better not to increase dividends for a few years to get the ratio down rather than to reduce dividends immediately. That's bad for the stock price, and we are still working for the stockholders.

Now that we've agreed on what business we're in and we've established goals of an equity ratio of 6.5%, an ROE of 16%, an ROA of 1.04%, and a dividend payout ratio of 25%, all we need to do is figure out how to produce it, presuming we're not already at or above those levels.

Identifying a Peer Group

The first thing to do is identify a peer group of eight to 10 banks that is similar in size to our bank, demographically similar (none will be perfect), and that produces the kind of earnings that we want for our bank. We shouldn't choose a peer group of losers so we'll look good by comparison. Instead we'll find a group of high performers. These are the people we can learn from. This is the class we'll want to be in. We'll send away for their annual reports. When we get them, we'll put them safely away. The following chapters will describe what to do with them.

SUMMARY

Many managers spend too little time setting goals in the beginning of the management process. At a recent shareholder's meeting, a bank CEO announced return on assets and return on equity goals for his bank. It was the first time he had publicly expressed his bank's targets. When asked by a shareholder to say when he expected to reach those goals, it appeared he had not yet given that part of his plan much thought. He said no time had been established for just when they expected to achieve those earnings goals. That statement changed those goals from goals to nothing more than a wish list.

Goal setting is critical and expected achievement times are also critical. Without a time factor, no one can ever be accused of failing. "We've still got the same goals, we just haven't achieved them yet."

Without solid specific goals set within stipulated timeframes, we really don't know where we're headed or when we might expect to get there. In this management environment we don't need a plan because we don't know where we're going. Quite obviously, this is not the way to get things done. High performing banks don't accomplish outstanding earnings by drifting along aimlessly hoping for the best. The entire process begins when we establish realistic aggressive goals which are to be achieved within a reasonable timeframe.

2 ASSET LIABILITY MANAGEMENT

During 1979, the prime rate changed 17 times beginning the year at 11.5% and ending the year at 15.25%. Prime dropped to 15% at the beginning of 1980, then it changed 11 times by April 2nd reaching 20%, it changed 12 more times by July 25th falling to 11%, and then it rose 18 times reaching 21.5% by year end. Prime changed 27 times during 1981 both rising and falling and ending the year at 15.75%.

There were no bank managers at that time who had ever experienced anything remotely like that before. No body of knowledge or experience was available on which to draw. America's bankers rode a wild roller coaster of interest rates. They couldn't steer it, they couldn't control it, they didn't know where it was headed, and they couldn't get off. Out of necessity, asset liability management was born to control net interest margins while general interest rates were changing.

An asset is considered "rate sensitive" if it carries an adjustable rate or is due to be repriced or mature within a specified time period. Rate sensitivity is concerned with the opportunity for interest rates to change. If we have more loans than deposits that have an opportunity to change rates, then when general interest rates go up, our net interest margin improves because our interest income goes up more than our interest expense.

Before getting any deeper into this subject, we should briefly examine how to determine the rate sensitivity of various assets.

MEASURING RATE SENSITIVITY

Federal funds are repriced every day. Loans tied to prime generally have their rates change when prime changes. Some may be contractually repriced monthly, quarterly, or even semiannually, adjusting to what prime is on the change date. Any loan that is paid off presents the banker with an opportunity to reinvest the money at current rates. Government bond rates don't change so they are not rate sensitive until the bond pays off, at which time the entire principal may be reinvested at rates then available. Some mortgage-backed securities are secured by adjustable-rate mortgages on which the rates change once a year on a pre-determined date. These securities may also have an annual rate cap, most often 2%, which limits the amount by which the interest rate may change.

If we want to determine the volume of assets that are rate sensitive within a six-month timeframe, we would simply add up the following:

- federal funds sold;

- all securities due to mature within six months;

- any other money market instruments due to mature within six months;

- and all loans tied to prime that can be adjusted within six months; and all scheduled principal payments on all loans that are due within six months.

This figure will tell us how many dollars of assets have an opportunity to reprice within six months.

To accomplish the same thing on the liability side of the balance sheet, we would add up the following:

- federal funds purchased;

- money market accounts;

- any other accounts with adjustable rates;

- CDs, repos, and consumer term deposits due to mature within six months;

- and any other liabilities with repricing opportunities within six months or less.

Perhaps a quick look at Table 2.1 will help clarify all this. The sample bank portrayed in this example has $55 million of rate-sensitive liabilities and $50 million of rate-sensitive assets. That means the bank has a negative gap of $5 million. The bank is "liability sensitive" because it has more liabilities repricing than assets.

Presuming the total rate sensitive assets and total rate sensitive liabilities in our bank do not equal, we will have a six-month "gap." If there are more liabilities than assets repricing, we have a "liability-sensitive" bank within the six-month timeframe. If more assets are repricing, we have

Table 2.1   Rate Sensitivity Measurement

Non-Earning Assets:	$10,000	Demand Deposits:		$14,000
Fixed Rate Loans:	30,000	Fixed Rate Deposits:		24,000
Fixed Rate Investments:	10,000	Rate Sensitive Deposits:	55,000	
Rate Sensitive Loans:	45,000			
Rate Sensitive Investments:	5,000	Total Capital:		7,000
Total Assets:	$100,000	Total Liabilities:		$100,000

This Bank is 5% "Liability Sensitive"

an "asset-sensitive" bank. If we think about it a little, it appears that a liability-sensitive bank will benefit from falling interest rates. As rates fall, more deposits reprice downward than loans. Interest expense falls more than interest income falls, and margins (the difference between the two) increase.

The opposite happens when rates rise in a "liability-sensitive" bank. Interest expense goes up more than interest income and earnings decline. This is what happened at the end of the 1970s as all interest rates rose sharply. Thrift institutions were paying increasingly higher rates for the then new six-month money market instruments and their fixed-rate mortgage portfolios did not change. Interest expense went up more than interest income. Margins and earnings totally disappeared. This became known as "interest rate risk."

INTEREST RATE RISK

Interest rate risk is the risk that earnings will fall if interest rates move. If a bank's rate-sensitivity position is perfectly balanced, theoretically, there is no interest rate risk because there is no gap. An equal amount of assets and liabilities will be repriced, and margins will remain unchanged. For many banks, asset liability management means managing maturities of assets and liabilities so there is no gap. They usually try to do this by managing maturities of the investment portfolio. If our choice of security is determined by a desire to match the maturities of certain liabilities, we will not be getting the top yields available. If a positively sloped yield curve exists, we can increase yield by choosing securities with longer maturities. When we extend the maturities of our assets, our bank becomes more "liability sensitive" than it was. With a positively sloped yield curve, we can increase earnings by becoming more liability sensitive. It is tempting but dangerous. Some measure of sensitivity balance must be maintained, and the fine-tuning is generally done with investments, not loans.

However, many small banks just don't seem to bother, and as long as general rates don't change more than 2% a year, they can probably do very well following this attitude of "benign neglect." However, if we ever have another year when rates change 6% to 10% in 12 months, those banks could experience extreme problems.

In the annual reports of banks we will find some form of "rate sensitivity report." It will generally list months one, two, three, six, twelve, and over twelve. Month six will hold the totals of months four, five, and six. Month twelve will contain the totals of months seven through twelve. These reports will list the totals of all rate sensitive assets and rate sensitive liabilities that will have an opportunity for rate change in the months listed. The bottom line on these reports will usually show a cumulative or running total of the bank's gap or net rate sensitivity position.

We shouldn't let this report lull us into a false sense of security. It is anything but precise. Measuring a bank's rate sensitivity entails a number of uncertainties and represents a best guess in at least some areas.

Rate Sensitivity Measurement Problems

Even if contractual maturities are equal in whatever timeframe we are measuring, there are a lot of things that happen every day to invalidate many measurements. First, people prepay loans. That means some funds show up for reinvesting that we did not expect. Every day some people sell their homes and buy new ones. The old mortgage gets paid off, and we have a certain amount of money to reinvest. We might add that these people invariably prepay their mortgages precisely when we wish they wouldn't. The same thing happens with consumer loans. Somebody decides to trade in his/her old car, and we have some un-expected principal to reinvest. While loan prepayments vary from time to time, place to place, and at different rate levels, we have found that there are from $.80 to $1.20 of unscheduled principal prepayments for every $1.00 of scheduled principal payments on mortgages. In periods when rates have fallen dramatically, prepayments on mort-gages can equal several times the amount of scheduled payments as millions of people refinance their mortgages to lock in lower interest rates. We have similar prepay-ments on consumer loans. Over six months, that can change our gap measurements significantly.

Other things also happen. The money we are scheduled to receive on a loan may not be reinvested in a similar loan if there is no current demand for such loans. So even though our maturities are balanced, our reinvestment op-portunities are uncertain and assets might shift at maturity from high-yielding consumer loans into low-yielding gov-ernment notes. Our margins can suffer even though there is no gap. It's also possible that a 90-day CD will mature the same month as a five-year government note, and if they are for the same amount, these two items seem to balance each other. However, 90 days ago when we put on the CD, rates were lower than today, and five years ago when we bought the note, rates were higher. Even though our maturities are balanced, the CD will renew at a higher rate and the bond at a lower rate. We have no gap but interest expense in-creases, interest income decreases, and our margin con-tracts. Because the assets and liabilities that seem to balance each other had different start dates, we cannot assume our net interest margin won't be affected, even though we seem to be balanced.

When interest rates change, they don't all change at the same rate. Over time, the prime rate seems to average about 115% of the jumbo CD rate. This means if we have

$100 worth of loans tied to prime and $115 of jumbo CDs, when market rates move our net interest margin won't change. Although we have a technical "gap," we have no rate risk. These relationships are not precise.

When prime changes 1.0%, three-month treasuries might change .75%, three-year treasuries .60%, five-year treasuries .55%, and ten-year treasuries .50%. We must take into account these different change rates experienced by different assets and liabilities when attempting to forecast the impact a general change in interest rates might have on our bank's margins.

Money market accounts tend to change much less than prime. If a bank had a zero gap with equal deposits and loans repricing, it might appear there is no interest rate risk. However, if prime goes up, the rates on the loans move further than the rates on the deposits and margins increase. When prime falls, so do margins and earnings. This means if we had a bank with nothing but money market accounts and prime rate loans, we'd have to stay very liability sensitive to eliminate interest rate risk. On the other hand, because bankers can control the rates they pay on money market accounts (within limits), they are able to protect their margins (within limits) by simply not moving their money market rates in step with other rates. As general rates change, rates on treasuries, agencies, T-bills, and fed funds also move less than the prime rate. While nobody can know for certain exactly how much each of these rates will change the next time prime changes, some estimate must be made when planning a strategy involving the bank's rate sensitivity position.

The Customer and Interest Rates

Adding to the bankers' problems of adequately protecting margins is the intelligence of the average customer. When interest rates go high enough, several things begin to happen to the bank's balance sheet. People begin to transfer money out of regular savings, money market accounts, and NOW accounts, and put it into higher yielding, longer term deposits, or other investment options. Rate-sensitivity measurements can't predict this. During periods of unusually high rates, corporations reduce all unnecessary borrowing and reduce balances in their checking accounts. Some adjustable-rate loans may stop adjusting upward when they hit ceilings or usury law limitations. When rates are high, everyone wants adjustable-rate loans and long-term, fixed-rate deposits, exactly the opposite of what the banker would like. When rates are low, people want fixed-rate loans and short-term deposits. When rates are low, customers refinance their higher costing fixed-rate loans and move out of adjustable-rate loans into fixed rates. Every time a consumer makes an intelligent choice concerning rates and terms of loans or deposits, it hurts bank earnings. There is nothing we can do about this. We should expect the customer to make financially sound decisions. We must learn to live with it and adapt our plans so our bank makes money anyway.

No matter how hard bankers try to anticipate the effect changes in interest rates will have on our margins, we can't plan for all the changes that will take place on our balance sheet as customers switch from one type of account to another, and change from one maturity to another, on both loans and deposits. Changes on the bank's balance sheet that improve the customer's earnings do so at the expense of the bank.

Obtaining Rate-Sensitivity Data

Still another problem for the banker in trying to control rate sensitivity is obtaining the data needed in the form needed from existing computer systems. Few systems tell us how many dollars of installment principal is due to pay out three months from now as well as what interest rate will be going off. If the computer systems can't give us the data we need, we're forced to make estimates.

Of course, we haven't even mentioned new deposits and profits, both of which offer a new pricing opportunity for new funds. If we receive a new checking account carrying no interest expense and we invest those funds in anything at all, we've increased our net interest income and slightly changed the rate sensitivity of our bank. All new deposits change the bank's maturity schedules. The same happens when we invest next month's earnings the month after that. Profits are new dollars that are now available to be invested in whatever maturity we choose.

VARIABLES BEYOND THE BANKER'S CONTROL

There may be a bank out there someplace that has figured out all these variables and that has a computer system capable of delivering all of the needed data. We haven't found one. The problem is that once we get by the contractual maturities, we are faced with a whole set of variables, all of which are beyond the banker's control. Does this mean we should throw up our hands and give up trying to measure rate-sensitivity, gap, and interest rate risk? Not at all; it would be foolhardy to do so. It just means we should recognize the limitations of such measurements. We must be constantly alert to changes within our bank and never depend on a particular rate-sensitivity position to protect our margins for very long. By the time we have assembled all of the data and made all of the estimates necessary to measure our bank's sensitivity, the situation has changed. We have to constantly reassess where we are and where we think we should be.

Mainly because deposit rates move less than loan rates, most consumer banks should be somewhat liability sensitive to protect earnings in a changing rate environment. Ideally, the bank will be on one of the many asset liability computer models that enable bankers to predict net interest margins into the future. These programs allow "what-if" scenarios to be tested in varying rate environments.

In many banks only the chairman of the asset liability committee can understand the computer model. This is a dangerous situation. If the president of the bank doesn't understand the assumptions that have been fed into the model, he or she has no idea of the reliability of the forecasts. If rates move suddenly and bank earnings collapse, it will be too late to cross-examine the report writers. Everyone who uses the income forecast reports should understand all of the assumptions that are part of the model. Does the model assume changes in volume for each asset and liability category? If so, how much, and is it realistic? Are forecasts internally consistent? For example, in a rising rate environment, people take funds out of savings and other low-rate deposit accounts and transfer them to higher yielding term deposits or even investments outside the bank. If we are projecting income in a higher rate scenario, a change in time deposit balances should also be built into the model. Rates don't change in a vacuum. And if the model assumes prime will increase 2%, then all other rates cannot also increase 2%. Fed funds, T-bills, and just about everything else will increase less than 2%. The computer model should reflect this, and those using the model's forecasts should be aware of the assumptions being used.

EXPRESSING RATE SENSITIVITY

A few words on expressing rate sensitivity seem in order. There are several ways to measure a banks's rate-sensitivity ratio. If we divide rate-sensitive assets by rate-sensitive liabilities, we obtain a ratio. Anything greater than 1.00 means the bank is "asset sensitive." A ratio of exactly 1.00 would mean the bank is perfectly balanced in whatever time period is being measured. Anything less than 1.00 would indicate the bank is "liability sensitive." It's a popular method because we can quickly observe whether the bank is asset or liability sensitive, and it easily lends itself to establishing numerical policy limits. There is, unfortunately, one serious flaw in depending on this particular ratio.

Suppose we have a $100 million dollar bank with $30 million in rate-sensitive liabilities and $20 million in rate-sensitive assets. That gives us a rate-sensitivity ratio of .67 and a negative gap of $10 million.

Across the street is another $100 million dollar bank with $60 million in rate-sensitive liabilities and $40 million in rate-sensitive assets. That gives us a rate-sensitivity ratio of .67 and a negative gap of $20 million. Thus we have two banks of the same size and the same rate-sensitivity ratio, but one has double the gap or double the problem of the other. If rates change, one bank will be much more affected than the other, even though both had the same rate sensitivity ratio. We shouldn't use ratios that can mislead us and do us harm. Expressing the rate sensitivity ratio in this way doesn't accurately measure the size of our problem.

If we measure our gap as a percentage of total assets, then we can arrive at a specific number. We can still easily identify a liability sensitive bank (one with a negative percentage) from an asset-sensitive bank (one with a positive percentage). In our example above, using this method the first bank would have been –10% and the other would be –20%. We would rather focus on that kind of indicator. We still can tell immediately whether we're asset sensitive or liability sensitive, but with this ratio we have a more accurate idea of the size of the gap.

Eliminating Interest Rate Risk

In some banks, management tries to hedge mismatched maturities to completely eliminate interest rate risk. They may try any of several instruments. Perhaps the simplest is the interest rate swap.

The Interest Rate Swap

Briefly, this is how an interest rate swap might work. We would enter into an agreement with a money center bank. Our bank would pay a fixed rate of interest on $10 million (or whatever nominal amount we agreed on) to the money center bank. The money center bank would pay us a variable rate of interest on $10 million. No principal changes hands between the money center bank and our bank, only the interest payments pass between us. In this case two banks swap interest payment streams. Why would we exchange interest payment streams?

Suppose a borrower requests a $10 million dollar five-year, fixed-rate loan. Our bank is already too liability sensitive so we don't want any more fixed-rate loans. We could arrange an "interest rate swap" for $10 million with a money center bank. The borrower pays us a fixed rate on $10 million. We are paying the money center bank a fixed rate on $10 million. In effect, our borrower is paying a fixed rate through us to the money center bank from which we receive a variable rate. We are receiving a variable rate even though we booked a fixed-rate loan. Thus, we are able to give the customer the fixed-rate loan that he or she wanted while we receive a variable rate. Seems simple enough, until we do the arithmetic.

The borrower will pay us a rate that is higher than the rate that we will pay the money center bank. However, on day one the money center bank will not pay us the same variable rate as the fixed rate we are paying to them. Five-year fixed-rate loans carry higher rates than adjustable-rate loans. Adjustable rates are short-term rates. With a positively sloped yield curve, a five-year rate might be 2.0% to 3.0% higher than a 90-day rate.

While there are many different kinds of swaps, when we get done sorting it all out, we will often be paying about 2% (200 basis points) more than we are receiving. Whatever index our adjustable rate is tied to—be it prime, LIBOR, or something else—it will be a short-term rate. The amount that we will pay over what we will receive will depend on the term of the loan and the index our rate is tied to. We may also make payments quarterly and receive them semiannually, further widening the spread between what we are paying and what we are receiving.

If we start out 2% behind on a five-year loan, prime (our index) must go up 1% a year for five years for us to break even. By "break even" we mean, where we would be if we had made the loan without the swap. Payments on our variable part of the swap transaction must average 2% higher than they are on day one. If prime increased 2% on day one and stayed there for five years, we would break even. Seldom will we come out ahead. We haven't even mentioned the money that we'd lose in a falling rate environment when our borrower refinances his loan at a lower rate and we still have to pay the higher fixed-rate obligation on the swap. When interest rates fall, borrowers commonly refinance their fixed-rate obligations at lower rates. Not only has the short-term rate we are receiving from the money center bank dropped, widening the spread between what we are paying and receiving, the higher fixed rate we were receiving from our customer has disappeared completely. This type of swap is designed to protect banks in a rising rate environment.

If all loans carried a 2% rate protection fee, our bank would never make any money at all. Some bankers love interest rate swaps but we, obviously, do not. Interest rate swaps represent interest rate risk insurance. For them to make sense to us, the borrower would have to pay a rate that is about 2% higher than he'd pay without the swap. Those who favor using swaps would probably point out that so long as the rate on the loan is at least 2% higher than the rate being earned on those funds right now, the bank is better off making the loan with the swap than doing nothing at all. If the bank can manage its rate-sensitivity risk some other way, it is even better off by making the loan without the swap. If we buy insurance to cover every risk, we won't make any money. Managing risk, not eliminating it, is what bankers get paid to do. No risk, no reward.

Financial Futures Contracts

Futures contracts probably make sense for farmers. If we're raising corn in the spring, we'd like to be able to lock in a price for harvest time. We might buy a contract to sell in October at some specific price. Now we're committed to sell, and somebody else is committed to buy at a specific price, regardless of where prices may be in October. The person who agrees to buy sets a price that he thinks will be better than the market price in October. The farmer would rather lock in a modest profit than take a chance on selling at a loss, so he pays for this futures contract. Over time, the farmer comes out behind because he doesn't get to set the price. It's a little like betting against the house in Las Vegas. So long as they get to establish the rules of the game and set the price, they win.

A financial futures contract is an agreement to buy or sell a specific financial instrument at a specific price at a certain time in the future. Financial futures carry even more risk than swaps. On every financial futures contract there must be a settlement. Somebody must win and somebody must lose. There are several dangers with futures. The first danger is basis risk. This risk is the result of the futures contract changing in value at a different rate than the item being hedged; it might even change in the wrong direction. We can't buy futures contracts to cover deposit rates, although brokers will tell us deposit rates are tied to T-bill rates, so a T-bill futures contract will work. Sounds logical but deposits don't move in step with T-bills, especially if we don't choose to price our deposits off T-bills. Additionally, deposits and treasuries may or may not move at the same rate. It is not necessary to use futures to protect the margins of a commercial bank. We believe futures contracts carry more risk than they cover. They represent expensive and unreliable insurance.

If we buy a futures contract priced like a 10-year treasury, it will change in value as rates go up or down based on the change in value of a ten-year treasury with an 8% coupon. Our contract will be similar to an agreement to buy (or sell) in the future an 8% 10-year treasury at some set price. If we have a contract to buy at today's price, and interest rates fall between now and settlement date, the value of a 10-year treasury increases as does the value of our contract. If rates fall, the market value of government securities go up. If our bank is asset sensitive, to protect against a drop in rates we would agree to buy government bonds in the future at today's price. Then, when rates go down, and margins in our asset sensitive bank shrink, we can buy governments at below market prices or simply sell our futures contract at a profit.

Unfortunately, anybody who followed this very logical strategy toward the end of 1981 when prime was falling from a high of 21.5% could have lost money on the futures contract instead of making money as anticipated. This came about because the yield curve was changing from a negative slope to a positive slope, short rates were falling, but long rates were actually rising. For a short period of time, as prime was falling, rates on long bonds were rising. After the yield curve reestablished itself in a positive slope, the entire spectrum of rates slowly settled lower. But at that particular time of settlement on the futures contracts, the bank could have lost money on the contracts, and by being asset sensitive, they could have had their margins fall as well. Nobody needs a double hit in times like those.

Some smaller thrifts failed at the time because they had invested heavily in GNMAs at the high rates that were then available. That alone would have been fine, but many of the best known economists on Wall Street were predicting that the prime rate was about to go up further from 21.5% to 25%. Thrifts, which were very liability sensitive, had their earnings destroyed by the unprecedented run up in rates. In that scenario the industry was worried about an extension of the rate trend upward, and many took measures to protect against still higher rates. The most professional advice went something like this:

> If rates go higher, all those high-yielding GNMAs will be under water, and we won't be able to afford the loss necessary to sell them and reinvest at still higher rates. In the meantime, our deposit costs will rise. We need an instrument that makes money in a rising rate environment. If we agree to sell securities in six months at today's prices, those securities will be depressed by the higher rates. We should buy a futures contract to sell at today's prices. We will be able to sell the futures contract at a profit if rates rise. That profit will offset the loss on the GNMAs, which we will then be able to sell and reinvest at higher rates. On the other hand, if rates fall, there will be a loss on the futures contracts but there will be an offsetting profit

on the GNMAs we're holding in our portfolio. We're protected either way.

Experts in a Wall Street firm advised bankers to use treasury futures because they behaved more predictably and had a better, more liquid market than GNMAs futures did at that time.

It was done, rates fell, the treasury futures went way under water and surprise, surprise, the GNMAs increased in value far less than anticipated. The difference between the amounts the GNMAs went up and the futures contracts went down was great enough to put some S&Ls out of business.

The reason for this differential could have been anticipated by a banker who had stopped to think about it. Unfortunately, none of them had been through such a situation before so nobody really had experience in what to expect. When interest rates fell, people began to refinance their mortgages in wholesale fashion. As a result, the average maturity of the GNMA securities plunged. The market, realizing what was happening, priced the GNMAs as though they were securities with an anticipated life of only two or three years, not 10 or 12 years. The futures contracts represented treasuries with much longer fixed lives. In effect, thrifts found themselves hedging a two-year instrument with a 10-year instrument. Unfortunately, it doesn't work. They would have been heros if they had done absolutely nothing. Sometimes the most professional advice from outside the industry can prove disastrous when things happen that the outsider didn't anticipate.

Interest-Only and Principal-Only Strips

Two newer instruments are the interest-only strip and the principal-only strip. Some banks buy interest-only strips and principal-only strips to supplement income in a changing rate environment. If we can envision a mortgage amortization chart, we will remember that in the beginning, we pay mostly interest and a little principal, with that ratio reversing itself toward the end of the loan. An interest-only strip is simply the interest payment stream from a pool of mortgages. The payments are large in the beginning and get smaller as principal is repaid. We spread those interest payments out for 30 years, factor in an expected prepayment rate, and take the net present value of that payment stream using a current interest rate for the discount factor. If interest rates rise, prepayments will slow down so we receive more interest than originally expected and the yield goes up. If interest rates go down, prepayments will speed up as people refinance their mortgages, and the total interest collected goes down thereby reducing the yield.

It's important to remember that an interest-only strip is pure premium, and we may not get back the amount that we paid for the security in the first place to say nothing of the anticipated yield. If all of the mortgages in the pool pay off tomorrow, we receive no more payments at all and we write off the entire balance of our interest-only strip. We don't think that these should be used in a bank because they carry too much risk. Whether the pool will experience lower prepayments depends as much on the rates on the underlying mortgages as it does on current market rates. It also depends on what part of the country those mortgages come from. Some areas always prepay faster than average and some always prepay slower. It is unnecessary to gamble with these instruments and, in our judgment, the opportunity for loss is too high for the possible gain. Even if we could accurately predict when rates will change and by what amount, we cannot accurately predict what impact that change will have on the average life of every mortgage pool in America, keeping in mind that they are all different. It seems the risk involved with interest-only strips is greater than the risk of doing nothing. At this moment, bank regulators seem to agree.

Principal-only strips are another matter. Principal-only strips are similar to interest-only strips, except we now receive the stream of principal payments. These are small numbers in the beginning and get larger as we get deeper into the life of the mortgages. On these, we know that we're going to collect all of our principal. Our yield may go up or down if prepayment speed changes from the anticipated rate when the instrument was priced. If prepayments increase and we collect our money faster, our yield improves because the time the money is outstanding has been shortened. The opposite can also happen, but we will eventually be paid all of our principal. If all loans pay off tomorrow, unlike the interest-only strip in which we receive nothing, with a principal-only strip we receive all outstanding principal immediately. The effect would be a tremendous one-time profit because all of the discounted amount would be received at once. We want principal-only strips to pay faster than anticipated, thereby increasing the yield. These securities carry less risk than interest-only strips, but their yields and prepayments behave too erratically to be a reliable hedge against changing rates.

Bank examiners have been trying to understand rate sensitivity for a long time. It's difficult to accurately predict what will happen to margins in a changing rate environment, not only for all of the reasons outlined above, but also because it takes a little experience with a customer base to know what all of those individual people are likely to do when rates change. Some markets are much more sophisticated than others. Generally, we wouldn't suggest relying on a "feel" for something, but after all of the most careful measurements and forecasts are made, we still need a sense of what changes are likely to take place on our balance sheet in our particular bank as rates change.

Measuring Third Decimal Place

Perhaps it's not necessary to be precise to the third decimal place in trying to measure rate sensitivity. Consider a $100 million dollar bank with $10 million in money market accounts and a $5 million negative gap. That means we have $5 million more in deposits than in loans repricing. If all rates go up 1%, we have $5 million times 1% or an increase of $50,000 more in interest expense than interest income as a result of the change. But wait a minute. Suppose we choose to raise rates on our money market accounts only one-half percent instead of a full one percent. One-half percent of $10 million is $50,000. We have solved our mismatch problem by simply limiting the amount of rate increase on our money market accounts. When prime goes up one full percent, it is not unusual for money market accounts to go up only one-half percent. This happens all the time. When money market accounts constitute a larger portion of our balance sheet, we can control margins somewhat by limiting the movement in rates on these accounts. So, in our example, a bank that appeared to be 5% liability sensitive did not experience any lost income when rates went up 1%. Not what we might expect.

However, this is a double-edged sword. When prime is falling, it is not possible to keep up with the degree of change in money market account rates. If prime falls one percent we may only be able to drop money markets one-half percent. We better be liability sensitive when this happens.

SUMMARY

This whole business of predicting changes in margins caused by changes in general interest rates is a very imprecise art. We have not been through enough interest rate cycles without Regulation Q to accurately predict changes in a bank's balance sheet. There are some asset liability managers in very large banks who think they can do this. They base their belief on data collected from one business cycle. That is not statistically reliable. It's a little like the young couple who have one child and assume that they now know all about children. They will believe this until they have a second child, at which time they will discover that there are at least two kinds of children in the world.

We cannot afford to totally ignore the rate sensitivity of our bank. If we have anything but a money center bank, our best guess is to keep our bank somewhere between a negative 5% and a negative 10% of total assets at the six-month timeframe. We know banks differ. Those with a higher dependence on jumbo CDs and repos are less flexible in pricing, and those with a higher concentration of money market accounts are more flexible. Those with more flexibility can better overcome bigger gaps and mistaken forecasts. We should test our banks future margins by playing "what-if" games on our asset liability computer model, factoring in not only what we think future rates will be, but also what changes they will cause on our balance sheet.

During a period of rising rates, expect our bank to become progressively more liability sensitive. This happens because increasing loan demand is forcing us to buy money. This generally takes the form of jumbo CDs, reverse repos, and federal funds purchased. More depositors are choosing longer-term higher yields, and others are transferring out of savings and NOW accounts and transferring into money market accounts or other money market instruments. We can't fight the trend. When rates peak and head back down, we'll want to be more liability sensitive. It would be counterproductive to pay still higher rates on long-term, fixed-rate deposits to become less liability sensitive just before rates fall. We sometimes tend to take actions designed to protect ourselves against what just happened yesterday instead of what's likely to happen tomorrow.

Finally, we shouldn't try to make money on rate changes. As soon as we do, we become a speculator. No bank strategy should depend on interest rates moving in some predetermined manner. We should make our money on margins, fees, noninterest income, and low overhead. Smart bankers don't try to hit home runs by accurately predicting when, how much, and in which direction interest rates are about to move. More importantly, we can't let people who are working for us gamble on interest rates, even if they try to justify their actions by calling it a hedge. Over time, we lose more than we win.

Once in a while, when earnings are good, we may get a feeling that we are absolutely sure that rates are about to fall. We want to buy some long-maturity securities to create securities gains or to improve margins after those rates have indeed fallen. It's okay to do it so long as it is done in moderation and we don't need those gains to meet plan or some other goal. We shouldn't do it if we can't afford to take the losses, especially if our forecast turns out to be wrong. Even the small time gambler knows that we never bet money that we can't afford to lose because if we do, we'll lose. Gamble for bonus money, not for required earnings. We can bet our vacation money, but we should never bet our food money.

Knowing full well that a zero gap will almost never protect our margins, we should use our asset liability computer model to estimate what gap level does best protect our margins. We'll try to operate our bank within the limits we deem to be safe, and if we are outside those limits, we'll try to slowly get back into line by making more or less fixed-rate loans, adjusting maturities on securities, or trying to change our liability mix. If we are using no system at all for projecting our margins, under "normal" conditions with a positively sloped yield curve, a rule of thumb is to be 5% to 10% liability sensitive at the six-month maturity level. This won't work for all banks and it won't work in all rate environments. It will, however, work much better than doing nothing and hoping rates don't change the wrong way while we're in charge.

Finally, virtually every commercial bank we've ever investigated was more asset sensitive than their rate-sensitivity measurements indicated. It is not unusual to find a bank with a reported negative gap that is actually asset sensitive. This happens when banks underestimate anticipated loan prepayments and assume that if the prime rate goes up, all other rates go up an equal amount. In 1980 when many asset liability committees were first formed, the person preparing the reports was most concerned about dramatic increases in rates because that was what had just happened to cause so much damage. As a result, any biases they built into the rate-sensitivity report were designed to protect the bank in a rising rate environment. For example, they might include a portion of their demand deposits as "rate sensitive" because when rates go up, people tend to draw down demand deposit balances. But what about when rates go down?

For all of the above reasons, many banks are less liability sensitive or more asset sensitive than their reports indicate. As a result, many banks keep all of their adjustable-rate mortgages and sell all of their fixed-rate loans. This needlessly hurts earnings. They might also pay higher rates than necessary on long deposits and buy shorter-term securities than they need to. All of these things unnecessarily hurt earnings because the bank's rate-sensitivity reports are not as accurate as they could be. Anyone using the bank's rate-sensitivity reports as a tool when establishing pricing or maturity policies should be absolutely certain that he or she understands all of the assumptions that go into that report. Otherwise, daily decisions about which loans to keep and which to sell and how to price deposits can continually limit earnings unnecessarily.

Chapter 2

3 STRATEGY

When we first formed an asset liability committee back in 1981, we were not exactly sure just what such a committee was supposed to do. After examining reams of data, we eventually agreed that our primary job was to maintain or improve our net interest margin. We did exactly that and it worked wonders.

We had been using a peer group of eight bank holding companies to measure our own performance. These were all multibillion-dollar multibank holding companies, none of which included money center banks.

When we examined data from the best performers in our peer group and compared it with the poorer earners, we were forced to discard several preconceived ideas that we had held.

For example, there was no positive correlation between loan deposit ratio and return on assets. We had supposed that a company with more of its assets invested in higher yielding loans, as opposed to lower yielding securities, would produce better earnings. It still seems logical, but we couldn't find any data that showed high loan deposit banks actually produced better earnings. It is possible to run a high performing bank with a low loan deposit ratio or a poorly performing bank with a high loan deposit ratio. The loan deposit ratio is merely the relationship between total deposits and total loans.

It's possible that a well-run bank might make more money if it had a higher loan deposit ratio than it would with a lower one, but there was no way to be sure of that.

Since that time we've dug a little deeper into this question.

Anytime we want to test a banking theory, we like to study pre-flood Iowa. Iowa is one of the last states that think small is better. There are approximately 550 banks in Iowa serving a total population of less than three million; about the size of Chicago. At last count, they had only three banks with total assets over one billion. If we eliminate those three, we have a fairly large sample of similar sized banks and identical laws and regulations.

We began by listing all banks in the state in order of return on assets. We had about 50 to 55 banks in each 10% grouping. Then we merged all the banks in each 10% grouping together and obtained what looked like ten banks. They were then listed on a graph, best to worst by ROA, and there was no positive correlation with the loan deposit ratio. In fact, there was a slightly negative bias that suggested banks with slightly lower loan deposit ratios actually performed better.

In any event, a high loan deposit ratio is not a prerequisite to good earnings. There are probably very few bankers who would readily accept this idea because it doesn't seem logical. Nonetheless, what are we to conclude if we can find no positive correlation between earnings and loan deposit ratio?

Although this doesn't seem logical, we could consider two 100-million-dollar banks, one with $40 million in loans, and one with $80 million in loans. Which bank will have higher overhead, higher charge offs, and a higher loan loss reserve? The bank with more loans.

In any event, there is nothing in this book that requires anyone to accept this idea, and none of our strategies depend on it. If we can't accept the idea that more loans don't necessarily lead to better earnings, that's okay.

CAPITAL RATIO

Different banks seem to have different beliefs about what constitutes a proper capital ratio. All we really need to remember is the higher the capital ratio, the more difficult it is to produce a good return on capital, and the easier it is to produce a good return on assets. The reverse is also true. The lower the capital ratio, the easier it is to produce a good return on capital, and the more difficult it is to produce a good return on assets.

If we compare our own bank's performance to a peer group, whether we're focusing on ROA or ROE, we should make sure the peer group banks have capital ratios that aren't too much different from our own.

There are really only five factors that affect bank income: interest income, interest expense, charged-off loans, noninterest income, and overhead. Interest income and interest expense have historically presented the best opportunities to affect earnings. If we can charge a higher rate on a loan, the extra income falls straight to pretax earnings because nothing else is affected. It doesn't cost any more to service a 12% loan than a 10% loan. It doesn't cost any more to service an 8% certificate of deposit than a 7% certificate of deposit.

Table 3.1 relates to a major bank holding company's recent annual report. It shows a 10-billion-dollar bank holding company and indicates that a one-half percent increase in net yield on earnings assets equals $46,426,000. If this bank had a return on assets of .80, it earned $83,945,000. If it could increase the yield one-quarter of one percent on all its loans and investments and reduce the rate paid on all

Table 3.1   The Bank

Average Total Assets:	$10,493,137,000

A one-half percent increase in the net interest margin equals:

A. $46,426,000
B. 29% of Total Salaries ($159,505,040)
C. 113% of Total Occupancy Costs ($41,134,801)
D. 151% of Total Computer Costs ($30,681,662)

deposits by one-quarter of one percent, it could increase before-tax earnings by $46 million dollars! That equalled 113% of total occupancy costs. If we could figure out how to run this company without buildings; if we could eliminate all heat, light, taxes, insurance, rent, depreciation, leasehold improvements, maintenance, and janitorial services, it wouldn't equal a one-half percent change in the net interest margin. If we could figure out how to run this bank without computers, the people who run, maintain, and program them, and the buildings that house them, it wouldn't equal a one-half percent improvement in the net interest margin.

The after-tax benefit of this improvement would change a good performing bank with an ROA of .80 into a high performer with an ROA of 1.07. What is easier to do, charge an extra one-quarter of one percent on loans and pay one-quarter of one percent less for deposits, or run the bank without buildings?

Many banks seem to launch cost-cutting programs every two or three years and perhaps they should. The primary focus of the next decade will be on the reduction of overhead, particularly salaries. This will be true in almost all industries. However, adjusting interest rates has a much more dramatic impact than reducing most overhead items. Although we are totally in favor of cost control programs, while these campaigns are taking place, it is very important that somebody keeps an eye on margins and makes sure that we don't save a few dollars by eliminating a report that's needed to monitor some part of the net interest margin. It's possible to build a comprehensive plan designed to reduce overhead, to put the plan into operation, and to complete it successfully, only to discover at the end that earnings haven't improved because the net interest margin slipped 15 or 20 basis points, while overhead was reduced by a lesser amount.

Improve the Net Interest Margin

All of this leads us to conclude that the number one goal of asset liability management is to maintain or improve the net interest margin. If our bank offers the highest rates on deposits and the lowest rates on loans, then we will inevitably find ourselves working for the poorest performing bank in our marketplace.

Marketing people, loan officers, and branch managers don't want to hear this. They want to offer the best prices. When bankers meet people at the country club, the golf course, or the Rotary meeting, it's more fun if they can offer the highest rates. Then we don't have to explain anything. We don't have to sell anything. In fact, we can be pretty independent. We can adopt this kind of attitude toward people, "If you want the best rates, you have to deal with me, but I'll be nice to you anyway." It's much more fun than trying to explain why they should use our bank even though they can get a better rate someplace else.

Pricing Our Products

This brings us to our main rule of high performance banking. If the number one goal is to maintain or increase the net interest margin, then the rule is, "Pricing our products is more important than EVERYTHING else."

For most of the past 40 years, bankers were not allowed to price their products. State usury laws set maximum rates that banks could charge on all kinds of loans. Almost all banks charged the maximum. Federal regulators set a limit on how much interest banks could pay on deposits. Most banks paid the maximum allowed. If banks didn't have too many employees and didn't make too many bad loans, it all seemed to work out fine. Bankers complained for years and lobbied for deregulation of interest rates. Finally, legislators listened: usury laws were changed or eliminated; Regulation Q, which limited the amount of interest banks could pay, was eliminated; and the nation was faced with an entire industry whose senior executives had never been trained to price their own products.

Until the end of the 1970s, most banks charged and paid similar rates. Business development consisted of giving away toasters and blankets. In the early 1980s with interest rates generally deregulated, bankers could finally compete on the basis of price. Unfortunately, banking is one of those businesses where you can't make up for low prices with higher volume. Capital constraints don't allow unlimited growth. If our bank has a 7% capital ratio, we can pay a higher rate on our deposits, increase our size 16%, and we now have a capital ratio of 6%. How long can we continue that strategy?

Most banks formed asset liability committees at that time, and they proceeded to build a very scientific pricing mechanism for determining rates on deposits. The committee met on Tuesday morning, and they checked the rates being paid by all the other banks in town, then they would set their own rates.

Price and Product

Maybe this is a good place to talk a little bit about price. Do most people make most of their decisions based on price?

Many bankers seem to think they do, but if people made all of their choices based solely on price, then we'd all be driving Yugos or Ford Fiestas. Why buy anything else if a Yugo will get you back and forth to work cheaper? Why does anybody buy a Buick? Why do people buy Cadillacs? Certainly not for the low price. Why would anybody at all buy a Mercedes or a Rolls Royce? Clearly, there are factors at work besides product cost. Do we all buy all of our clothes at Kmarts? Why not? Do we all use Bic pens? Why do so many bankers use Cross pens? It can't be price. Why can convenience stores, with higher prices, flourish right next to supermarkets?

People don't buy Toyotas and Hondas because they cost less. Toyotas and Hondas possess superior workmanship. They don't break down as often as other makes. Men don't buy suits at Nordstrom's because they cost less. They buy them there because they receive excellent service in the store, the suit will fit when they get it home, and if anything at all goes wrong with the transaction, it will be fixed to the customer's satisfaction.

People will pay for quality and for value. As the average standard of living in America rises, people will become somewhat less concerned with price. They can afford better and they want better. However, the general public is not stupid. They will not pay extra if they are not getting something extra. A company cannot charge a quality premium if it does not deliver a quality product.

In all of the above cases, while price may be a consideration, it is not the deciding factor. People are making decisions while considering style, size, color, image, dependability, comfort, convenience, looks, service, and any number of other things besides price. The simple fact is that most people make most decisions based on many things, and price is seldom the overriding factor. In any market, there is only one bank with the highest deposit rates. Why don't they have all the deposits? Why are people going to the other banks? Why does anybody at all go to the bank with the lowest rates? Obviously, something is affecting depositors' choices besides price. People are getting something from those other banks besides rate.

If we run a bank and the only thing that we have going for us is price, we will have a major problem. People who come to our bank for price will be the first to leave for price. The day we can't match the highest rate in town, we've got troubles. Price-driven banks have fewer options than other banks; consequently, they are less able to exercise control over their bank's fortunes.

Most bankers demonstrate their insistence on competing on the basis of price in their advertising. Compare bank advertising with other advertising. A few years ago, we saw happy families singing, dancing, and driving to their favorite burger place to a chorus of "You deserve a break today." We saw shots of happy people doing all sorts of lively and fun things in the great outdoors, refreshing themselves with a long drink of their favorite cola, while off camera we are being urged to "Join the Pepsi generation." Stylish model-type women in the sleek and sexy red sports cars were seen heading out to meet sophisticated dates for a fantastic evening while the announcer told us that, "The night belongs to Michelob."

What are all these people selling? Is anybody talking about price? Does Michelob tell us their six-pack costs less than Heineken? Of course not. These people aren't selling price.

In contrast, examine the typical bank ad. "Our money market account has an interest rate of 5.25% with an annual yield of 5.33%. Interest is paid from day of deposit to day of withdrawal, $1,000 minimum deposit required, substantial penalty for early withdrawal." If we set out to design the most unimaginative and boring advertising known to mankind, could we top that? Why do we do it? Bankers aren't stupid. Why can't we find something better to say about our companies? Why can't we hire the same people who do ads for Coke, McDonald's, Pepsi, Michelob, Miller or Chevrolet? We never give our customers a reason to do business with us. All we can talk about is higher rates and the banker across the street is saying the exact same things. All of our ads look alike. How is the customer supposed to distinguish one bank from the other except for the rates, if anybody can remember all the numbers, or even wants to. It seemed more interesting when banks were giving away toasters.

We should pass a rule in our banks that says nobody can work in marketing if they started in banking. People who begin their careers in banking don't have the right mindset to work in advertising or marketing. Their idea of a real snappy ad is to list the yield first and then the interest rate to make their pricing look better. We should hire marketing people who have never set foot in a bank voluntarily. If they suggest an ad that mentions price, we'll fire them immediately and hire new people. They're probably impostors.

Competing on the Basis of Price

It is said that the general who chooses the battlefield will win the war. Why then do banks choose to compete on the basis of price? It is the one battlefield on which we can't win. The bankers across the street may not be able to match our branch locations or the quality of our personnel, but they can match our price. They aren't going to sit there quietly and watch us drain deposits out of their bank without responding. As soon as our competitors become aware that they are losing deposits, they'll raise their rates to stem the flow. Now we're both paying more for what we had before anyway and neither side wants to back down. It's a little like two adversaries lobbing grenades across the street at each other, both doing damage, neither able to win, and neither party willing to retreat. When we decide to compete on price, we have chosen the one factor that anyone can match. We can't win on price in banking. We must develop a strategy in which we compete on the basis of super service, not price.

If it seems we have devoted an inordinate amount of space trying to convince the reader not to compete on price, it is no accident. Competing on the basis of outstanding service rather than price is the underlying strategy of this entire book. Many accounting firms and some management consultants will claim that more people make their decisions based on price because they cannot determine any other differentiating factors. With commodities, this may be true. If people really can't identify any differences among banks, they very well may make choices based on price alone.

ESTABLISHING RATES

When establishing rates for all new loans and deposits, bankers are determining next year's net interest margin. No matter what pricing strategy a bank adopts, for it to work, everyone in the bank must understand and support it. When we are retained to conduct an earnings improvement workshop, we try to gather as many members of management as possible so when we are finished, everyone has seen the same data, heard the same ideas and understands the resulting strategy. Only then can we hope to have everyone pulling in the same direction. Results are usually immediate.

If we condense a bank's income and expense report into its five major segments—interest income, interest expense, provision for loan losses, noninterest income, and overhead—it may be easier to visualize what happens in a bank (see Table 3.2).

Table 3.2 Income and Expense Report

	Bank A	Bank B	Bank C	Bank D
Interest income	220,589	194,829	100,217	94,942
Interest Expense	(113,897)	(97,691)	(53,732)	(42,643)
Net Interest Margin	106,692	107,138	46,485	52,299
Loan Loss Provision	(9,952)	(6,439)	(3,185)	(2,608)
Other Income	17,883	19,567	6,750	8,566
Overhead	70,585	67,466	31,945	(35,508)
Before-Tax Income	44,038	42,800	18,105	22,749

We can stare at those numbers long enough to get a headache. They don't really deliver a very clear message. However, if we check Table 3.3 in which the same figures are presented as a percentage of average total assets, it becomes much easier to make comparisons. It also makes it easier to develop a profit improvement strategy. If performance goals are set in terms of return on assets, we can express each of the above five factors as a percentage of total assets and immediately see how each affects the return on assets. It also allows us to compare our bank's earnings with our peer group's and to make comparisons against our own bank from year to year.

Table 3.3 Percent of Average Total Assets

	Bank A	Bank B	Bank C	Bank D
Interest income	9.53	8.97	9.71	9.83
Interest Expense	(4.92)	(4.50)	(5.21)	(4.42)
Net Interest Margin	4.61	4.47	4.50	5.41
Loan Loss Provision	(.43)	(.30)	(.31)	(.27)
Other Income	.77	.90	.65	.89
Overhead	(3.05)	(3.11)	(3.09)	(3.68)
Before-Tax Income	1.90	1.96	1.75	2.35

In Table 3.3, each bank can quickly determine in which areas they excel and which areas present the best opportunities for improvement. It also forces us to focus on a limited number of general areas when developing a strategic plan.

Net Interest Margin

First of all, the net interest margin (the difference between interest income and interest expense) is the biggest single number in each bank. That means there is greater opportunity for gain or loss in that single number than in any of the others. For that reason, we have always stressed high margins as essential to superior earnings. However, if our bank pays rates that are average (in the middle of the pack) and charges rates that are average, then our margins will be average. Many bankers do just that and focus instead on reducing overhead. In fact, most of the emphasis in the 1990s has been on reducing overhead. This will continue; "re-engineering" has become the buzz word of the decade. Some banks do an unbelievable job of holding down costs. Overhead is the next biggest number of those listed above so it also contains a large potential for change.

A high performing bank should produce a return on assets that is 30 to 40 basis points above average. All of the banks represented in Table 3.3 are already above average. Yet, is it possible to produce an average net interest margin, average loan loss allowance, and average noninterest income, and to join the ranks of the superstars through expense control alone? Probably not. It would require an overhead figure that is so superior to the average, only a handful of banks could expect to achieve it. It is not impossible, but it is extremely difficult.

The best route to consistently high performance is to outperform the peer group by a modest amount in each category. Consider Table 3.4 as a possible set of three-year goals.

Table 3.4   Three-Year Goals

Outperform Peer Group By:	
Interest Income	15–25 Basis Points
Interest Expense	15–25 Basis Points
Loan Loss Provision	5–15 Basis Points
Noninterest Income	10–15 Basis Points
Overhead	15–25 Basis Points
Total	60–105 Basis Points

If we can produce before-tax earnings of 60 to 105 basis points above our peers, we'll have a super bank unless we cheated in choosing our peer group. It is easier to do a little better in every category than it is to do a huge amount better in one category. Someone once said, "To a man who has only a hammer, all problems look like nails." If our bank has a superstar in charge of operations, and everyone else is average, we might try to excel by containing overhead. We still don't think it's the best approach to take. We don't need super people to produce a high performing bank. We can do it with average people and a super plan.

In any event, if we get used to comparing our bank to our peers by concentrating on the five major areas as a percentage of total assets, we can quickly identify and attack the areas that hold the most promise for improvement. Any strategic plan should be stated in terms of these categories.

We successfully concentrated on the net interest margin and produced outstanding and immediate results. Nonetheless, even with great margins, no bank can afford to ignore the other three areas. Earnings improvement can be achieved in each category.

Let's try to summarize all these concepts. First we'll identify a group of banks in our state, most, if not all of which exceed our bank's return on assets and return on equity. This can be done in several ways. Companies such as Sheshunoff, Ferguson, and SNL Securities produce databases that can be purchased. Lacking that we can simply obtain the annual reports of the banks we want to use.

The next step is to compare our bank with the others to determine where we are in relation to the high performance group. We'll determine how many dollars of earnings we would make if our bank was at the average of the high performing group, and from that we'll determine where to put most of our efforts. We will typically start by producing a set of 35 to 40 bar charts on which we will compare our bank with the high performing group. We'd start with the five main categories of income and expense and then get into more detail in the individual categories.

For example, if the subject bank was average in the areas of interest expense and loan quality, above average in non-interest income, but below average in interest income and overhead, we'd concentrate more on the last two categories. We'd dig into overhead to determine if the problem was in salaries and benefits, occupancy expense, or other overhead items. We might further compare average salary per employee and average assets per employee to try to determine whether we have too many people or we're paying too much to the ones we have. Then we'd try to find detailed ways to solve those problems. These are discussed more fully in subsequent chapters. This is when the strategic action plan is developed.

Years ago, business consultants advised us to do more of what we do best. For example, if our company has two products, product A which produces 90% of revenues, and product B which produces 10%, there will be a natural tendency to try to bring Product B up to the volume of Product A. This is bad thinking, we were told, since an 11% increase in Product A equals a 100% increase in Product B. Since the customer already clearly prefers Product A, we should concentrate our energies there, because it will be easier to increase Product A.

Benchmarking, on the other hand, believes we should compare our performance with other companies in the same business who are outperforming us. Then we should concentrate our energies in those areas that suggest the best opportunities for improvement. That's what we've been describing in this book.

Finally, the late Edward Deming, who after World War II showed the Japanese how to produce better cars, televisions, and just about everything else, had a different view. Deming was a statistician by training, and he believed every step of every process should be continually improved. While American car companies might average 100 changes per year, the Japanese would average a thousand.

From all of this we must develop a strategy for our bank. We believe we should begin by using benchmarking to accurately determine where we are and to help determine where we would like to be. We should first concentrate on those areas of the bank where we are the furthest off the group average, but we should simultaneously be trying to improve everything else. This is not as difficult as it may sound because the same people are not involved in every area. The senior lender can be trying to improve credit quality at the same time the operations officer is trying to reduce overhead and the branch administrator is trying to improve service.

We should establish goals for each of the five primary areas of the bank's income statement: interest income, interest expense, provision for loan losses, noninterest income, and overhead. Those goals should be expressed as a percentage of average total assets. They can be expressed as the final number we are trying to achieve or as the amount of change we are trying to produce.

For example, if our bank's overhead equals 3.75% of total assets, our goal might be to get overhead down to 3.25% of total assets or to reduce overhead by .50% of total assets.

It might also be necessary to produce a change of this size over two years.

Once those goals are established, we should identify the people who will be responsible for each of them. Along with them we would then determine exactly what will be done in each area to produce the desired changes. The people responsible for executing the plans must then report back to the president or senior management group on the progress being made. These reports should be made monthly or at least quarterly.

The management process seems to break down most frequently at the control phase. A good plan is developed but it doesn't get executed because nobody followed up to see that the details of the plan are enacted and the desired results are achieved. Management must follow up to see that everything is done and that it is working. If changes have been made but they have not produced the anticipated results, then the plan must be adjusted.

The rest of this book is devoted to examining some of the means we might employ to achieve the various improvements we'll need to produce higher earnings.

4 INTEREST INCOME

The typical officers' loan committee consists of six to 10 senior lenders who meet once or twice a week to review loans that are above the lending limits of individual loan officers. They might spend one-half hour or more discussing the credit quality of the borrower and eventually decide to approve the loan. They then spend about 30 seconds determining the interest rate to be charged. Most of the time it will be prime plus one percent. Why do so many loans go on at prime plus one? Perhaps everybody recognizes that the local borrower should pay more than General Electric, but once they get past prime, most loan officers don't go much further.

Most loan committees spend too little time on loan pricing. It's almost as if the whole process was beneath them. In one office of our bank, we have an investment officer who bids on certificates of deposit and municipal borrowings in increments of one hundredth of a percent. Loan officers generally think in much larger increments. Few banks have lines of credit priced at one and three-eighths over prime. There are prime plus one and a few prime plus one and one half, but nobody pays prime plus one and seven eighths. Why not? Loan officers don't think that way at most banks.

Loan officers usually charge their best customers too much and their poorest customers too little. They do not devote adequate attention to pricing. There is not a sufficient spread in loan pricing to properly reflect the differences in credit quality, and this seems to be true just about everywhere. Some banks use loan pricing models, but when the model indicates rates that the lending officers think are too high or uncompetitive, the model is commonly ignored.

Additionally, banks generally evaluate loan officers on credit quality (charge-off ratio) or new business development. Loan officers are seldom ranked or rewarded for charging higher interest rates. The attitude seems to be, "We're not responsible for the level of interest rates, what can we do?"

Some banks pay a bonus based on loan fee income generated. This is dangerous and should be closely monitored for two reasons. First, the person collecting the bonus should not be approving the loans, nor should any other officer who is in the program. The tendency is to relax credit standards just a little to collect the fee and earn the bonus. The second problem stems from the way fees and rates on loans are interrelated. The higher the points, the lower the rate. The lower the points, the higher the rate. If the loan officer is earning a bonus for collecting points, or fees, the tendency is to raise points and lower rates. This hurts the bank's margins, sometimes for a very long time. Any bonus program associated with commercial loans must be very carefully constructed and monitored, or it may produce unanticipated negative results.

We are generally opposed to paying a bonus to loan officers based on fees or volume. The tendency is always to relax credit standards or loan pricing just a little, and we don't want either relaxed, not even a little. We would make an exception to our negative feelings about bonus plans for loans in the case of residential mortgage loan originators because they don't get to approve the loans or set the rates, and the underwriting standards in the residential mortgage business are pretty well established. Credit quality and pricing can be controlled.

CREDIT QUALITY

We believe in high loan quality. Nonaccrual loans reduce the net interest margin, and problem loans cost five to 50 times as much to collect as good loans. A poor loan portfolio hurts earnings in several hidden areas of the income statement besides the standard "provisions for loan losses."

Table 4.1 examines what might happen if we could increase volume by 20% when we relax credit standards enough to double our charge-off ratio from four tenths of one percent to eight tenths of one percent. This is not the kind of thing we could accomplish by design. We don't turn down 20% of our loan requests now; so to increase volume by 20%, we'd probably have to do something besides relax credit standards. We might want to do those things anyway.

In any event, if we could increase volume 20%, Table 4.1 shows what would happen. In the first set of numbers, we collect $110,000 in interest income, assuming we charge an average rate of prime plus one, and we deduct $40,000 in chargeoffs for a net interest figure of $106,000. With the increased volume we collect $132,000 in interest income; but we experience charge offs of $9,600 and we lose the income that we had been earning on the extra $200,000 in loan volume. In this example, we assume the money to fund the loan increase came from our federal funds account. We either reduced the amount of federal funds we

Table 4.1   Proposal: Relax Credit Standards to Increase Loan Volume 20%

Prime: 10.00%
Federal Funds; 8.50%
Charge offs: .4% vs. 8%

Commercial Loans	$1,000,000
Interest Rate @ Prime + 1	×.11
Interest Income	$110,000
Less: Charge offs @ .4%	−4,000
	$106,000
Commercial Loans	$1,200,000
Interest Rate @ Prime + 1	×.11
Interest Income	$132,000
Less: Charge offs @ .8%	−9,600
	$122,400
Less: Federal Funds Income Lost	−17,000
	$105,400

were selling or increased the amount we were borrowing. In either case there was a cost for that money. If the new loans were funded by reducing the investment portfolio, then the cost should be the yield we were collecting on the securities that we had to sell, probably a return higher than federal funds. When we're all finished, we do more volume and make less money.

We can play with these numbers and make any assumptions we want, but we invariably discover that we don't make any more money when we relax credit standards; we just do a lot more work.

We once owned a bank that had disproportionately large credit problems when we took over. There had been a sharp decline in the real estate market, and this bank had what proved to be too many land development loans. For the first three years it was like running a huge collection agency. Every officer in the bank had eight or 10 "work-out" loans that he or she was managing, and that was all we ever talked about. We were forever holding meetings with lawyers, bankruptcy referees, and desperate borrowers, not to mention with employees, auditors, and the bank examiners. We didn't have time to run the bank. We never had enough time to make customer calls, develop new products and programs, train officers and employees, or do any of the other things that are so much a part of a vital growing bank. These are the hidden costs of abnormally high delinquency rates. The whole bank is retarded. Once all those officers are free of the demands of chasing bad loans, they are capable of producing all kinds of great results. But that's hard to do when we're rushing from fire to fire.

If this isn't reason enough, we should remember that the leading cause of bank failures is bad loans. It's easy to blame economic conditions for bank problems, especially if it's our bank experiencing those problems. But, how do we explain why two banks in the same economic community produce very different earnings? One has administered its loan portfolio differently than the other. We have never seen a bank produce consistently high earnings with a high nonperforming loan ratio. If we are unfortunate enough to be managing such a bank, we should remember the first rule of first aid; stop the bleeding. We could write an entire book on how to turn around a bank that is loaded with bad loans. Suffice it to say that step one is to stop making more loans like the ones we're struggling with. This is easier said than done.

Making Good Loans

Most loan officers believe that they are making good loans. Maybe we have to hire somebody from outside to bring a different perspective; but if we do, we should check the nonperforming ratio of the bank they're coming from. If it is not a lot better than ours, don't bother. The other thing we must do is to say out loud, "We are going to stop making loans that turn into problems!" We should say it often and forcefully. We shouldn't give raises to the worst offenders. We must occasionally reduce or take away loan limits. The president should sit in on all loan committee meetings, and he or she shouldn't make loans so he or she can be as critical as necessary. We can't be afraid to turn down an occasional loan that might have been okay. The only way to be sure we never turn down a good loan is to approve them all. We should set specific goals for delinquencies, charge offs, nonperforming loans, and any other category we want to monitor. We must review, revise, and enforce our loan policy.

Reviewing and enforcing loan policy doesn't seem like a very effective way to increase interest income, but most bank we've examined with a bad loan portfolio had a reasonable loan policy that was being largely ignored. If more than 5% of our loans are exceptions to policy, our policy is not being followed. A senior officer should review all branch loans. Everybody in the bank should know that we are watching closely and expect changes. We would explain why a lower charge-off ratio means more profits for the bank and ultimately, better service for the community, even if it means less volume. When we are all done, if we still have a stubborn loan officer complaining that we can't make loans without having charge offs, we'll tell him we don't need executives repeating childish slogans. We don't expect to eliminate all charge offs, just most of them. Our charge to our officers should be, "You can get on the bandwagon or get off, but you can't drag your feet."

Nonperforming loans carry a zero interest rate, and we don't need a degree in mathematics to realize that if 5% of our loan portfolio is paying zero interest, the overall yield is going to be seriously hurt. We shouldn't pursue volume by relaxing credit standards.

Why are we so adamant about never relaxing credit standards? Because it's easy to do when pursuing volume, especially if we run a bank for a holding company with centralized investment management. If we are in a position where the only way we can make budget and earn a bonus is by making loans, then we will have a major problem if the local economy won't supply us with sufficient high quality loans. We either have to make fewer loans this year, which might cost us our job, or put on marginal loans, which could cost us our job next year or the year after. Most people in this position will probably decide to worry about next year. This keeps us employed for another year but hurts the company in the long run. We have a similar problem when rates fall. This generally happens when loan demand is falling. If our plan and bonus runs on loan interest income, we will need to put on more loans just to break even at a time when demand is weak. It creates too much pressure on loan officers to do things that are unsound.

Some bank managers insist on greater loan volume to make plan, then they are surprised when margins fall and charge offs increase. Just what do they think the loan officers are going to do to increase loan volume? Loan officers must relax interest rates and credit standards. Making calls on competitor's customers won't do it quickly. Are our bank's best customers going to leave us just because they were called on by a competitor requesting their business? Not unless the competitor offers a much lower rate or waives some collateral requirement. The borrowers who will move are generally the marginal credits. If we demand that our lenders produce instant volume increases, at least we should accept responsibility for the mess that's likely to follow.

PRICING LOANS

In Table 4.2 we assume that we can increase volume by 20% if we could reduce rates by one-half percent. We're not sure that we could increase volume that much, but if we could, and the increased loan balances were funded by reducing federal funds, then we'd end up making less money with more volume, and that doesn't even consider overhead. Again, we can play with these numbers using whatever assumptions we want; but unless we set out to make the numbers prove otherwise, we'll decide not to reduce rates.

Table 4.2 Proposal: Lower Loan Rates 1/2% to Increase Volume 20%

Prime: 10.00%	
Federal Funds: 8.50%	
Charge offs: 0.50%	
Commercial Loans	$1,000,000
Interest Rate @ Prime + 1	×.11
Interest Income	$110,000
Less: Charge offs @ .6%	−6,000
	$104,000
Commercial Loans	$1,200,000
Interest Rate @ Prime + 1/2	×.105
Interest Income	$126,000
Less: Charge offs @ .6%	−7,200
	$118,800
Less: Federal Funds Income Lost	−17,000
	$101,800

Some bankers make assumptions about which deposits fund which loans. If we assume commercial loans are funded by demand deposits or savings accounts, while installment loans are funded by higher costing term deposits, we can reach pricing decisions that seem to make arithmetical sense; but when we're done, earnings decline. We believe we should make those decisions based on what will actually happen in the bank. If we want to have a loan sale, we should determine precisely where the money will come from to fund the new volume.

Will we use federal funds? Will we sell some securities, and if so, which ones? The same holds true when buying loans. For example, if we have an opportunity to purchase a pool of loans, where will the money really come from? If we have federal funds available, we'd probably reduce "fed funds sold" and use that money to buy the loans. If we don't have enough, we may borrow federal funds to raise the money. In either case the real change in earnings will be the difference between the federal funds rate and the loan rates. If we don't like swapping short assets for long assets, we may decide to sell longer maturity securities to raise the money to buy the loans. Assuming that there is no profit or loss on the securities, the change in margin is now the difference in yield between the securities sold and the new loans, and we now have to add an amount to our loan loss reserve to cover the increase in loan volume. We should also consider future charge-off potential and the overhead involved if we have to service the loans. Aside from the origination and servicing cost, it doesn't really change the arithmetic if we purchase a pool of loans or make a batch of new loans in-house.

Setting Rates

Some loan officers will claim that they don't really set rates in their banks, the competition does. "If we don't charge rates similar to my competition, we don't make loans." This is one of those contentions that sounds logical and may contain a grain of truth. However, in real life experience it simply doesn't hold up. When we examine the average yield on loan portfolios in similar banks in the same marketplace, we frequently discover that one consistently does better than the other. Why doesn't the bank with the lower rate have all the loans? Obviously, there are other factors at work. In our experience we've found that rates charged are more a reflection of the philosophies of senior management than of external economic forces. Some lenders always want to offer lower than average rates. Some become accustomed to negotiating a slightly higher rate and deliver better service. They feel the higher rate is a reflection of their superior service. And some lenders always seem content to charge whatever it takes to keep the customer happy.

In summary, we should not compete on the basis of price. We should emphasize service, flexibility, helpfulness, professionalism, friendliness, courtesy, and a genuine desire to meet the customer's needs. If we need to negotiate, it should be on the length of the repayment program or the equity required. We should give fast, pleasant, and professional service and expect to be paid for it.

Be Consistent, Avoid Exceptions

We should be consistent and minimize exceptions. Every loan officer in the bank has at least some borrowers who pay less than they should because they've developed a close personal relationship. Maybe we play golf with Charlie on weekends, or eat lunch with him once a week at Rotary, or serve with him on some board, so he pays a little less than he should because we are not as persistent as we should be. Every officer in the bank with a loan limit has some of these and unless everybody is made aware of the situation and a tight lid is kept on such activities, we can discover hundreds if not thousands of "exception loans." It doesn't help to have good pricing standards if everybody is an exception.

We can't get into the habit of offering low rates to attract new accounts. After a while the low rates become "standard" for all new borrowers (what's good for your customer is good for mine) and then it starts leaking over to existing borrowers. Why should my dress store owner pay more than yours?

Money Sales

Don't have "money sales." It's virtually impossible to come out ahead with them. In Table 4.3 we assume that we are currently charging 12% on installment loans and that our cost of funds is 7.5%. We also assume our installment loan overhead cost is 2.0% and that we normally produce $10.0 million a month with rates at 12%. We have not factored in an expense for charge offs, increased loan loss reserve or advertising, or increased cost of servicing, but we legitimately could.

Table 4.3 also shows that if we reduce rates to 11% and don't increase volume we've lost $100,000 a year. If, at 11%, we increase volume 50% to $15.0 million this particular month we will have lost $20,000 a year. In real life we have to reduce loan rates more than 1.0% to produce a significant change in volume. Dropping installment loan rates from 12% to 11% won't change volume much at all. Installment borrowers are primarily interested in the size of the monthly payment. If we drop installment loan rates to 10% or 9.75% to get the public's attention, we now have to produce over five times our original volume just to break even. We can't do it. That much volume might not be available at any price.

Some might argue that loan overhead is present anyway so we shouldn't add an overhead amount. That assumption can get us into long-term trouble. It still costs money to take an application, obtain a credit report, print and mail a

Table 4.3   Break-Even Analysis on an Installment Loan Money Sale

12.00%	Current Loan Rate
7.50%	Cost of Funds
2.00%	Loan Overhead Cost
$10	Normal Monthly Volume

New Loan Rate	New Loan Volume				
	$10	$15	$20	$25	$30
12.00%	0.00	0.12	0.25	0.38	0.50
11.50%	−0.05	0.05	0.15	0.25	0.35
11.00%	−0.10	−0.02	0.05	0.13	0.20
10.50%	−0.15	−0.10	−0.05	0.00	0.05
10.00%	−0.20	−0.17	−0.15	−0.12	−0.10
9.50%	−0.25	−0.25	−0.25	−0.25	−0.25
9.00%	−0.30	−0.33	−0.35	−0.38	−0.40

coupon book, set the account up on the computer, and collect the payments. While we are putting new loans on, old loans are paying off and most of our overhead remains. If we price all of our products using the concept of adding only incremental costs, then the day arrives when all of our old products will be gone, and nobody is covering overhead. The only way we can legitimately use incremental costs in pricing a loan program, is if we can guarantee that absolutely nothing else will change, and that is almost never so.

Advertising managers like money sales because it's one of the very few times they can measure a response to their work. Customer contact officers like an opportunity to beat the market. Maybe there is some psychological value involved. We'd rather run a consumer loan campaign by giving something away and build a promotion around that. We might try a Bible, a dictionary and a cookbook, a car emergency repair kit, a watch, or a travel alarm.

Establish Written Rate Schedules

We should establish written rate schedules for all types of loans. Most banks have detailed rate charts for mortgages and consumer loans. The mortgage chart has various rate-point and maturity combinations. The consumer loan chart separates secured from unsecured, new car from used car, and 36-month from 60-month loans. But do we have equally detailed rates for commercial loans, and do we allow personal loans to be put on a note basis? Can a branch manager who must charge 12% on a new car installment loan put the same customer on a 90-day note for 8 1/2%? The branch manager probably can if he or she doesn't have anything to prohibit it; and if they can, some will. Banks should develop as detailed a rate chart for commercial loans as they do for all other types of loans. Secured costs less than unsecured; long-term costs more than short term; fixed assets can't be financed on an annual line of credit; monthly payment loans are put on installment; if we don't have these kinds of guidelines it's amazing what happens over time.

Once the rate schedule has been established, only the most senior officers should have authority to make exceptions. Imagine going into Sears, trying on a suit, and then saying, "I really like this suit and I'd like to buy it, but I can get it for $50 less at Wards." What does the salesman say to that? "Oh, okay, I'll sell it to you for $50 less." Of course not. He doesn't have the authority to change his company's prices. How many companies allow their salespeople to reduce prices whenever a customer complains? How long could they hope to stay in business if they did? What's so different about a bank? How can we hope to control interest income if every loan officer on the payroll has the authority to reduce price?

Using the Yield Curve

When pricing loans, we should recognize the yield curve. Longer generally costs more. Investment officers understand this. Money managers understand it. Investment bankers understand it. Stockbrokers understand it. Why is it so hard for loan officers to understand it? The prime rate is a short-term rate. If prime is 200 basis points above the 90-day T-bill rate, and our borrower is paying prime plus one percent on short-term notes, then he's paying 300 basis points above 90-day T-bills. If our borrower wants a five-year fixed-rate loan then he should pay 3% (300 basis points) above the five-year treasury note. More basis points (perhaps 60-85) should be added for the additional risk involved in longer-term credit. If prime is 4% above 90 day T-bills and our customer pays prime plus 1% on short-term notes, then he should pay the rate on five-year treasury notes plus 5% plus 60-85 basis points for a five-year fixed-rate loan. If all of this sounds much too high for the marketplace we can compromise some, but five-year fixed-rate loans shouldn't be written at prime plus one. We usually don't charge enough extra for longer-term, fixed-rate loans. Some bankers solve the problem by never making fixed-rate loans. That seems a bit extreme, but we wouldn't criticize such a policy having managed a bank through a 21.5% prime.

Fees for Unused Lines

We should charge fees for unused lines. Most banks have lines of credit established for contractors who never use those lines. Contractors need the lines to obtain bonding for contracts even though they don't need the credit. The bonding company wants the bank line available to help cover their losses if the contractor gets in trouble. That way the bonding company collects the premium, while the bank covers the first dollars of loss. When banks do this, their credit people normally "spread" the contractor's financial statements, compare the data to industry standards, analyze the figures, and prepare a written report. Then a loan officer or committee reviews all this and commits the bank to a certain amount of credit. All of this the bank does for absolutely nothing. Why? Perhaps because the customer expects it. Again, why? The customer doesn't expect to obtain bonding insurance for free. When the bank gives away something of value for free, the recipient generally believes it has no value.

We should also charge fees for loan commitments. People who buy homes are accustomed to paying "points" with a mortgage. More and more banks are collecting "points" for commercial loan commitments or for establishing annual lines of credit. (A "point" is one percent of the amount of the loan.) Historically, lawyers have claimed that once a loan commitment fee is collected, the bank is obligated to extend credit no matter what deterioration in the borrower's credit may have occurred. The easy answer for the lawyer is, "Don't collect loan commitment fees." Bankers and lawyers have since found ways to word commitment letters to protect the bank if the borrower's credit situation seriously declines.

Under the risk-based capital requirements, commitment fees need to be around 2% to produce an ROE of 15% or more.

Fees for Credit Cards

When pricing credit cards we generally consider the rate charged on purchases and cash advances, the interest-free grace period allowed, the annual fee, our charge-off ratio, and the overhead involved both in-house and from the outside servicing firm (if one is used). With this many variables in the equation, it is very easy to miscalculate.

Charge offs on charge cards are higher than any other type of credit because a customer with a $500 line can leave us with unpaid charges of $20,000 or more. The fee from the outside servicer is very complex because it covers our merchants and other merchants, our cardholders and other cardholders who use our merchants, and general overhead items. Sorting out the cost of handling a single cardholder is very difficult. When some customers pay zero interest because they always pay their bill in full, the average rate collected on the whole portfolio can be a lot less than the stated rate. If we have a low annual fee, we'll have a disproportionately large number of customers who pay no interest at all. If our delinquency rates are higher than normal, our in-house collection overhead will be higher than normal. If our credit quality is better than average, our cost of acquisition will probably be higher than average, because we'll be handling more applications to acquire a stated volume. It will cost more if we have to examine 200 applications to obtain 100 new accounts than it will cost if we only have to examine 150 applications to get 100 new customers.

Out of all this confusion we can be sure of several things. Credit cards have the highest charge-off rate of any other kind of bank credit. Credit cards cost more to handle than any other kind of bank credit. Unless our charge card rates are so low we lose money on them, people will not switch banks in large numbers to get better rates on credit cards. The top issuers of charge cards in the United States do not offer anywhere near the best rates. If people were concerned about rate, they wouldn't use a charge card in the first place.

The best thing we can do for our card customers is eliminate the grace period if our state allows it. Then the people who borrow don't have to subsidize the people who pay in full every month. It will allow us to charge a lower rate and collect the same amount of money. We shouldn't forget that a 25-day, interest-free grace period is really 55 days for the charges that come in the day after the statement date.

We could also afford to charge lower rates if our customer agreement says we can raise rates on the entire balance if, after giving the customer advance notice, he uses the card. Because card balances are outstanding for long periods and charge card rates don't change with other interest rates, we usually try to collect a high enough rate to cover future increases. If we could increase the rate on most of our balances, we could afford to accept a lower initial rate.

If we don't already have a charge card portfolio and we want to start one, it is very difficult to build up to break even volume unless we offer an interest rate so low that we lose money until we can increase it. If we plan to increase rates in a year or two, we should tell our customers at the outset so we can maintain our bank's reputation in the community. If we already have a portfolio, the easiest way to increase volume is to raise the credit limits of all customers with good paying records. We can also offer to skip a payment at Easter, Christmas, and "back-to-school" time. The interest is added to the balance outstanding.

Twenty years ago commercial loans always seemed to carry rates around 6% and installment loans were around 12% to 13%. Today many banks have allowed installment loan rates to drift lower, and they've come closer and closer to commercial loan rates. This shouldn't be. We cannot handle 36 payments for the same overhead as one payment on a commercial loan. Bankers no longer make anywhere near what they used to on their installment portfolios.

For some reason, when prime increases, installment loan rates very often do not. The reason is usually, "competition hasn't changed." That is probably because they are waiting for us.

Setting installment loan pricing should not be done by junior officers in the bank. There should be balance and consistency among loan rates. If the senior loan officer of the entire bank is a commercial loan officer, he or she will usually be more sympathetic to those loans. If he or she is a mortgage officer, mortgage terms and rates will be more competitive, and so it goes. Pricing both loans and deposits is sometimes done by the entire asset liability committee and sometimes by a committee composed of representatives of all loan divisions. Unless there are very specific pricing goals established, the most senior officers in the bank, including the president, should participate in the process. Only then can all rates move in a coordinated manner. If every division head doesn't understand what every other one is doing to achieve the net interest margin goals, there may be one or two trying to make up in volume what they lack in price.

We saw one bank raise rates across the board by one-quarter of a percent. This way they didn't have to explain to each individual customer why their credit standing had declined. They simply said that with prime this low our bank simply can't produce satisfactory earnings so we're raising rates across the board; nothing personal, we're just revising our pricing, hope you understand.

A bank might also pick a minimum rate it feels it can live with, such as prime plus one, and then target all borrowers paying less than prime plus one for an increase.

Many banks are now charging a "transaction fee" each time a borrower comes in to the bank for an advance under a line of credit or any time a note is processed. This can dramatically increase the yield on a loan without changing the rate. These fees, at this writing, have been generally running from $50.00 to $150.00 per note per renewal. This also cuts down paperwork as most borrowers plan their needs more carefully with the result being a reduction in paperwork.

Banks can also increase the yield on their commercial loan portfolio by changing the wording on their note form to provide for an increase in interest rate when the loan runs past due. In this case, "past due" means day one. If the note is due on the fifteenth, the rate goes up on the sixteenth and stays up until the note is paid or renewed. The amount of the increase in rate can be 4% or 5%. Since many borrowers don't come into the bank to renew their notes until they receive a past due notice, this rate increase can improve the yield on a loan portfolio by 20 basis points.It is necessary to consider usury laws if rates rise dramatically, but this can be done.

Many banks today establish their own "base rate" to replace the "prime rate." It can have any name, but the important thing here is that the bank has more control over earnings by not allowing the base rate to stay with prime. For example, when prime drops below 10%, the bank might float its in house base rate from 1% to 2% above prime. When prime is between 10% and 15%, the "base rate" might equal prime. And when prime exceeds 15%, the "base rate" might actually be less than prime.

Banks can improve interest income by improving the "earning asset" ratio. This is seldom obvious, but some banks earn interest on 95% of their total assets while others might be earning interest on only 87% of total assets. By reducing nonearning assets, the bank can improve interest income with no corresponding increase in interest expense.

This is usually accomplished by reducing the number of correspondent accounts in other banks, reducing cash and checks in process of collection, and by reducing the amount of Other Real Estate Owned. The gains can be significant and shouldn't be overlooked or ignored.

Most community banks maintain a certain level of fed funds sold and the amount is seldom questioned. Everybody knows a bank can improve earnings by reducing fed funds sold and investing those funds in higher yielding longer maturities, but they tend to take for granted that the current level is appropriate.

We once conducted a workshop for a billion-dollar bank that had $50 million in fed funds sold. We suggested that the amount, at 5% of total assets, seemed high and might be reduced. They said, "You don't understand, Al, we have a lot of large corporate and public demand deposits and our fed funds sold fluctuate between zero and $50 million. You just happened to hit a day when we were at the top."

I responded, "Well consider this. Suppose you reduced that by $25 million and invested in longer securities. If you can pick up 2% to 3% on $25 million, that equals $500,000 to $750,000 in increased interest income. Then you would let your fed funds float between $25 million bought and $25 million sold." Closely managing the bank's fed funds presents opportunities for increased interest income.

Investment income can be increased by extending the maturities of the portfolio. Everybody knows this, but many banks don't examine the issue often enough. It is not uncommon to find a bank investment officer who is so concerned about liquidity that he or she keeps the average life of the portfolio much shorter than it really needs to be. Extending the average life just one year can sometimes add a full percent to the portfolio's yield. In a bank with a loan deposit ratio around 50%, this represents a huge amount of money.

Investment officers can also increase yield by acquiring somewhat riskier assets. Government agency securities yield a little more than treasuries. Corporate bonds yield more than agencies, and mortgage-backed securities yield more than corporates; at least they do today. Senior management should decide what level of risk should be allowed in the investment portfolio. This will help the officer in charge produce the best earnings possible within those parameters.

While some improvement is usually available in a bank's investment portfolio, most interest income comes from loans, and the greatest opportunity for change is almost always in the loan portfolio.

The whole business of loan pricing is a touchy one. There are a number of ways to increase income on loans without actually raising the interest rates, and we've discussed several commonly used methods already. Many loan officers feel only they should be empowered to establish loan rates. They feel they must be free "to make deals." A little of this goes a long way. We're not really talking about a big difference here. We're not talking about 200 or 300 basis points. All we want to collect is one-quarter to one-half percent more. That's not a lot, but what a terrific difference it makes if everyone in the bank does it. People will pay one-quarter or one-half percent more if we give good service and treat our customers as we'd like to be treated. The critical question here is how we treat borrowers when they come into the bank. Do we make them feel as if they've done something wrong and we'll condescend to bail them out? Do we make them feel as if they're going to confession? Do we treat them the way a father treats his son when he asks for beer money? Or do we make them feel welcome and wanted? Do we go out of our way to be cordial and helpful? We should follow the Golden Rule: Treat borrowers the way we'd like to be treated, and the one-half percent doesn't mean a thing. Treat them poorly and it won't matter if we charge them prime minus two, they'll disappear when they believe it's safe to go.

Bankers must continually exert upward pressure on loan rates because borrowers, quite naturally, continually exert

downward pressure. If the banker does nothing, one borrower succeeds, then another, and another, and another,
and over time the yield on the entire portfolio slowly declines.

We have never seen a high performing bank anywhere
with lower than average loan rates. Getting higher rates is
easy to talk about but is not easy to do. If it were easy, all
banks would be high performers. Officers must be trained
to sell the bank's service instead of price. And then they
must be trained to deliver superior service. It doesn't come
naturally.

Later in this book in Chapter 9, we discuss outstanding
service in some detail. Generally, good service doesn't cost
more than poor service. In fact, good service often costs
less than poor service because there are fewer errors to
correct. If our bank always provides a level of service that
is noticeably better than our competitors, we'll be able to
charge rates and fees that will produce interest income results that are from .25% to .75% higher than our peers.

5 INTEREST EXPENSE

Improving bank earnings by reducing interest expense can have more immediate results than raising rates on loans. When a program is developed to improve interest income, the new pricing only applies to new loans. It may take three or four years for the results to be felt throughout the entire portfolio. If we reduce the rate paid on regular savings accounts today, it applies to the entire portfolio immediately, and we'll experience a substantial boost to earnings next month.

Banks establish rates on deposits about the same way they do on loans. The asset liability committee meets on Monday morning, checks the treasury yield curve, and the rates on various money market instruments. Then they examine the really critical material—the rates being paid by other banks up and down the street. If one asked the members of the committee how they establish deposit rates, they might offer something very complicated about spreads over treasuries and the federal funds rate. The truth is, however, the committee makes sure that the rates they are paying will maintain their relative position among their competitors. If their deposit rates are second highest in their market, they will adjust their rates to be just a little under the highest rate and above all the rest.

Sometimes a bank will try to maintain the highest rates in town. Almost nobody does that anymore, and if they do they won't admit it. Other bankers will always try to be third or fourth on the list and establish deposit rates that maintain that position. Some even try to always pay the lowest rate in their market. Although it sounds as if we're ridiculing the approach to set deposit rates relative to rates paid by all competitors, it has a certain practical merit if followed judiciously. Pricing deposits among competitors really means relying on their good judgement which may or may not be wise, but we can't blindly follow our competition into insolvency.

Some committees decide that they will be a certain number of basis points over or under the treasury yield curve. They do this until rates of competitors drift higher or lower in relation to the yield curve and their bank starts to get out of step with the others. Frequently, the system will then be abandoned for awhile. In late 1988 and early 1989, a negatively sloped yield curve was present. (Short-term treasuries produced higher yields than long ones.) In spite of this, most banks continued to pay higher rates on long deposits than on short deposits. Why? Force of habit? We're not sure. Some banks will key off a certain competitor. They'll always meet (beat) First National.

We once told a management group that we felt their rates on money market accounts were too high. They responded, "But Al, the First National has said they will always pay 20 basis points more than us on money markets." I answered, "That's interesting. What can you do about it?" When nobody replied I said, "That's right. You can't do anything. The only question is, do you want them paying 20 basis points over 6.5% or 20 basis points over 7%?" They could bid each other up and maybe somebody would eventually give in and the other would score a psychological win, but in the meantime both banks would be foregoing large amounts of potential profits.

Bankers who view deposit rates as a way of inflicting pain on competitors really shouldn't be running banks, and we shouldn't allow such people to obtain influential positions in our own banks. We work for the shareholder. We are entrusted with their capital and have a legal and a moral obligation to run our banks in such a way that the long-range benefit of the shareholders comes first.

If we think of the reduction of deposit cost as an opportunity to improve earnings, we might produce for examination a spreadsheet similar to Table 5.1. Here we assume our bank already has $100 million in money market accounts. We can also look at this as 100% of whatever we now have. In this example we also assume that if we increase balances slightly, the new deposits will be invested in federal funds at 9.0%. We establish money market deposits at 100 and a rate of 6.5% as ground zero. Table 5.1 shows the changes in net interest margin with various changes in rate and volume. Thus, if we stay at 6.5% and increase deposits $10 million or 10%, we make an extra $250,000 ($10 million times 9.00% minus 6.50%). This assumes that we somehow raise volume 10% without changing the rate we are paying.

Following the table down one line, we see that if we raise rates 10 basis points (one-tenth of one percent) but our volume doesn't change, all we've managed to do is pay an extra $100,000 in interest to a portfolio of depositors we had anyway. We can also see that we must increase volume a little under 5% to just break even on the higher interest expense of the entire portfolio. We must then ask ourselves if increasing the rate paid on our money market accounts 10 basis points will increase volume 4 or 5%.

If we don't already know the answer to that question, it is "No." Ten basis points is not noticed in the marketplace.

Table 5.1   Change in Income Due to Rate and Volume Changes (thousands)

6.50% Money Market Account Rate
9.00% New Funds Investment Rate
$100 Current Money Market Account Balance (millions)

New Rate	Money Market Account Balances (millions)							
	$100	$105	$110	$115	$120	$125	$130	$135
6.50%	0	125	250	375	500	625	750	875
6.60%	(100)	20	140	260	380	500	620	740
6.70%	(200)	(85)	30	145	260	375	490	605
6.80%	(300)	(190)	(80)	30	140	250	360	470
6.90%	(400)	(295)	(190)	(85)	20	125	230	335
7.00%	(500)	(400)	(300)	(200)	(100)	(0)	100	200
7.10%	(600)	(505)	(410)	(315)	(220)	(125)	(30)	65
7.20%	(700)	(610)	(520)	(430)	(340)	(250)	(160)	(70)
7.30%	(800)	(715)	(630)	(545)	(460)	(375)	(290)	(205)
7.40%	(900)	(820)	(740)	(660)	(580)	(500)	(420)	(340)
7.50%	(1,000)	(925)	(850)	(775)	(700)	(625)	(550)	(475)

Neither is one-quarter of one percent. Very few people will move for that amount. At one-half percent advantage, we might expect to see some deposit movement, but very little. As Table 5.1 shows, raising money market rates one-half percent increases interest expense $500,000 if volume doesn't change. With that increase in rate we have to increase volume 25% to break even. We must now ask ourselves if we can increase volume by 25%. Again, we doubt it because our competitors won't let us. As soon as they see any significant deposit loss, they will meet our rates and the game will be over; unless, of course, we want to raise rates still higher, or they do just to teach us a lesson. There is no way to notify the public that we are paying higher rates without also telling our competition.

Table 5.2 examines what happens if we adopt a reverse approach and consider reducing rates. If we reduce rates on our money market accounts by 10 basis points and balances don't change, we'll save $100,000. Will balances change if we drop rates one-tenth of one percent? No they will not, at least not in our experience. Generally, rates seem able to move about one-quarter percent up or down with virtually no change in balances. As Table 5.2 shows, if we dropped rates 30 basis points and balances declined 10%, we'd still be money ahead.

Well, what are we to make of all this? We really don't want deposit balances to decline, but we shouldn't avoid the possibility at any cost. Our suggestion is usually to reduce money market deposit rates about five basis points a week until we notice some movement in the balances, then move rates back up a little and hold there for awhile. We should not assume that we must always maintain some special position with our competition. We can experiment a little and see what happens. The potential rewards are great since changes affect the entire portfolio.

Table 5.2   Change in Income Due to Rate and Volume Changes (thousands)

6.50%	Money Market Account Rate
9.00%	New Funds Investment Rate
$100	Current Money Market Account Balance (millions)

New Rate	Money Market Account Balances (millions)						
	$100	$95	$90	$85	$80	$75	$70
6.50%	0	(125)	(250)	(375)	(500)	(625)	(750)
6.40%	100	(30)	(160)	(290)	(420)	(550)	(680)
6.30%	200	65	(70)	(205)	(340)	(475)	(610)
6.20%	300	160	20	(120)	(260)	(400)	(540)
6.10%	400	225	110	(35)	(180)	(325)	(470)
6.00%	500	350	200	50	(100)	(250)	(400)
5.90%	600	445	290	135	(20)	(175)	(330)
5.80%	700	540	380	220	60	(100)	(260)
5.70%	800	635	470	305	140	(25)	(190)
5.60%	900	730	560	390	220	50	(120)
5.50%	1,000	825	650	475	300	125	(50)

We should remember that our competitors are also trying to maintain a certain position on the rate table. If we are a major player in our marketplace, they can't reduce their rates if we won't reduce ours. Nobody wants to move first. They're watching us as closely as we're watching them; and if we drop rates, they may not respond immediately because they're not sure what we are up to. But sooner or later it will occur to them that we are maintaining our deposit base at a lower price than they are.

Table 5.3 assumes that we have some place to put additional money market deposits at a higher yield than federal funds. In this case, we don't need to attract as many new deposits for the numbers to make sense. But we have to be sure of a few things before we proceed.

Is the new use of funds really new, or is it something we're going to have anyway? For example, if we always do $5 million a month in installment loans, are we saying the new money market deposits will be used for new installment loans? That's not valid. We'd have had those loans anyway. They shouldn't be used as an excuse for paying higher rates on money market accounts. If we really do have an opportunity to obtain new assets, the correct question should be "What is the most economical way to fund these assets?" It should not be, "Should we raise money market rates to fund these new assets?"

Let's assume the following: our bank has $100 million in money market accounts at 5.5% and $5 million in federal funds sold at 7.5%. We have an opportunity to acquire an asset that gives us a net yield after overhead and chargeoffs of 9%. We believe that if we raise rates on money market accounts from 5.5% to 5.9%, we can increase deposits by $5 million. The question is should we raise money market rates and increase deposits, or eliminate the federal funds sold at 7.5% and use that money to acquire the asset?

Table 5.3 Change in Income Due to Rate and Volume Changes (thousands)

6.50%	Money Market Account Rate
10.00%	New Funds Investment Rate
$100	Current Money Market Account Balance (millions)

New Rate	Money Market Account Balances (millions)							
	$100	$105	$110	$115	$120	$125	$130	$135
6.50%	0	175	350	525	700	875	1,050	1,225
6.60%	(100)	70	240	410	580	750	920	1,090
6.70%	(200)	(35)	130	295	460	625	790	955
6.80%	(300)	(140)	20	180	340	500	660	820
6.90%	(400)	(245)	(90)	65	220	375	530	685
7.00%	(500)	(350)	(200)	(50)	100	250	400	550
7.10%	(600)	(455)	(310)	(165)	(20)	125	270	415
7.20%	(700)	(560)	(420)	(280)	(140)	(0)	140	280
7.30%	(800)	(665)	(530)	(395)	(260)	(125)	10	145
7.40%	(900)	(770)	(640)	(510)	(380)	(250)	(120)	10
7.50%	(1,000)	(875)	(750)	(625)	(500)	(375)	(250)	(125)

Let's check the arithmetic. If we simply exchange one asset for another, 7.5% federal funds sold for a new 9% asset, we increase the yield on $5 million by 1.5% or $75,000. Nothing else has to change so we're $75,000 ahead. If we pay 5.9% on $105 million in deposits instead of 5.5% on $100 million, we've increased interest expense by $695,000. Offset against that is a new $5 million in earning assets at 9% which equals $450,000. With interest expense up $695,000, interest income up $450,000, net interest margin goes down $245,000. Seems like an easy decision. But was it that obvious without the calculation? And do our people do the calculations on these decisions or do they follow their instincts? A certain mental discipline should be required of all officers making pricing decisions in any bank. We shouldn't rely on our instincts if a few simple calculations can clarify the choices. We should always look for the least expensive way to raise new money.

RATES ON SAVINGS ACCOUNTS

Nobody who wants high rates puts their money in passbook savings. People forgo the higher yields available to anyone who wants to actively manage their money because the savings account gives them something other than high interest. It gives them absolute peace of mind because they know that money is always immediately available, and it's earning some interest. The availability is very important, especially to people who may not enjoy some of the safety nets society provides. And nobody who uses the other savings instruments to manage their money will put money in savings accounts anyway. Savings accounts are almost like a batch of dormant accounts. They represent real rainy day deposits. It's hard to attract new ones. Most people who actually manage their money have already taken it out of banks and put it into some form of mutual fund.

Today most banks today charge fees on low-balance savings accounts. Although we like to charge a slightly higher rate for just about anything, we think each bank should supply some kind of deposit service for people with small amounts of money. That doesn't mean we can expect our paying customers to subsidize every financial service someone might want, but there should be some safe place where people of modest means can keep their money. We think regular savings accounts are as good a place as any if our bank is going to support the underprivileged in our community. Banks contribute to just about everything else. Why not keep one account available for children and welfare mothers and anybody else who has very little to deposit? We shouldn't do it because they may someday be rich and develop into profitable accounts. We should do it because we feel an obligation to supply financial services to the entire community.

We feel the same toward NOW accounts as we do toward regular savings. We don't think NOW accounts need to pay current market rates of interest. We don't think we can afford to pay enough to attract more than our fair share without getting all of our competitors to follow suit. People don't transfer transaction accounts as readily as time deposits. Accounting for outstanding checks, ordering new checkbooks, and finding a convenient office for weekly deposits make the hassle outweigh the benefits of a slightly higher rate on NOW accounts.

Consumer term deposits. Consumer term deposits represent the area where most rate differentials exist among banks. At any moment, some bank in the community is trying to lengthen maturities or shorten them, gain some new deposits to fund a loan promotion, or just out guess the direction of interest rates. About all we can say here is that if we want to offer higher than market rates to attract new deposits, we should do it with short maturities at the short end of the yield curve. It doesn't cost as much be-cause the rates are lower. If we guess wrong on the direc-tion of rates, it doesn't hurt as long. If our own customers switch maturities to take advantage of our promotion, it costs less when they switch from long to short than from short to long. Finally, if we must have a deposit promotion based on price, we might choose an odd-month maturity like seven months or nine months so those millions we have in six-month maturities quietly roll over without a rate increase. We really don't like deposit promotions based on price because we pay more for many deposits that we would have had anyway, and competitors will usually raise their rates somewhat while we're doing our thing to make sure that we don't take too many deposits from them.

Promotions for savings accounts. Instead of competing on the basis of price, we prefer sales contests for employees, awards for cross-selling, one or two gift promotions a year (teddy bears, VCR movies, video games), and just about anything else that is not based on price. Once our ads hit the papers with a one-of-a-kind stuffed animal, our com-petitors can't match it. Promotions also invigorate our staff. Being a teller can be very boring work if all we ever talk about are this week's rates which tend to blur with last week's and the week's before that. Anything that makes our bank look a little less boring to the public is also a plus. When it comes to excitement, bankers are just above law-yers and undertakers in most people's eyes. It shouldn't be that way, but we do it to ourselves.

The jumbo CD. The jumbo CD (over $100,000) is the one area of the bank in which the highest bidder usually gets the deposit. Some banks bid aggressively only if the amount is over one million. Most banks bid aggressively only if they need the money. Some bid aggressively even if they don't need the money if they have the customer's main demand deposit account. If a municipality or company maintains a million-dollar checking account (or a half million), we really don't want our competitor winning all the CD bids. It gives the appearance that the bank across the street is more interested in the customer than we are. On the other hand, the jumbo CD is a good way to raise a few million dollars extra when we need the money because we pay only for as much as we need and we don't pay more for deposits we would have had anyway at a lower price.

Suppose we have included on our balance sheet $100 million in money market accounts at 5.5%. We need an additional $10 million in deposits to fund new loan demand. Also, assume we believe we can raise $10 million in additional money market deposits by raising the rate to 5.9% or we can buy 90-day jumbo CD's at a rate of 7.5%. Which should we choose? We know $10 million at 7.5% equals $750,000. In the first situation, the real cost of the additional $10 million is not only the 5.9% percent on the new $10 million but also the additional .4% on the existing $100 million. It's necessary to figure out the incremental cost of the new money to determine its real rate. In this case, raising rates on the money market portfolio to produce new deposits looked like 5.9% percent but was really 9.9%. That means we actually paid 9.9% for the new money when it was available in the CD market at 7.5%.

Table 5.4 shows the incremental cost of new deposits when we are forced to pay a higher rate on an existing portfolio in order to attract some new money.

Some bankers try to adjust the maturities of their liabilities by occasionally paying higher rates on longer-term deposits. Trying to coax consumers into longer maturities can be very expensive. First of all, most consumers prefer shorter maturity deposits to longer maturities. Depositors will accept lower rates on shorter deposits because availability is more important than higher yields. This seems to be true no matter what the relative level of rates may be.

Table 5.4 Incremental Cost of New Deposits

Deposit Growth Realized	4.00% Existing Rate		New Rate Offered				
	4.25%	4.50%	4.75%	5.00%	5.25%	5.50%
5%	9.25%	14.50%	19.75%	25.00%	30.25%	35.50%
10%	6.75%	9.50%	12.25%	15.00%	17.75%	20.50%
15%	5.92%	7.83%	9.75%	11.67%	13.58%	15.50%
20%	5.50%	7.00%	8.50%	10.00%	11.50%	13.00%
25%	5.25%	6.50%	7.75%	9.00%	10.25%	11.50%
30%	5.08%	6.17%	7.25%	8.33%	9.42%	10.50%

It's much easier to coax consumers into short maturities than into long ones. We should really explore some other alternative if we are trying to extend maturities of liabilities. We must pay so much over market rates to get people to take longer-term deposits that we might discover the risk that we are protecting against is less than the cost of protection.

If we insist on paying deposit rates near the top of the market, we will have a very poor net interest margin. The only course left is to overcharge a great deal for loans and drastically reduce overhead. That means get rid of half of our tellers and customer service people, close all of our marginal branches, eliminate Saturday hours, return all overdrafts, truncate all accounts, and charge for everything. We can't charge for Chevrolets and deliver Buicks, we'll go broke. It doesn't work in banking or anywhere else. Before we choose to go for deposit volume at high cost, we must go on record as saying it makes no sense. Don't do it. It won't work. Read the rest of the book and we'll explain why.

SUMMARY

Interest expense is equivalent to the cost of goods sold in other kinds of businesses. Only bankers get to exercise some meaningful control over their cost of goods sold, or interest expense. Those who do not take advantage of this opportunity will not produce margins or earnings among the top 10% of their peers.

The difference in interest rates paid between average performing banks and high performing banks does not have to be great, but there must be a difference. It's simple arithmetic.

6 LOAN QUALITY

There seems to be little agreement among bankers about what constitutes an appropriate level of net charge offs to total loans. When banks fail, it is almost always because they made too many bad loans. Even so, many bankers seem willing to allow net charge offs to become dangerously high in their banks without feeling compelled to do anything about it. So with net charge offs, how much is too much?

If we take all of the banks in any state or region and list them in order of ROA, the best earners will have the lowest charge-off ratios. The banks with earnings records in the top 10% nationwide will have net charge offs to total loans well below one-quarter of one percent. Banks can have net charge-off ratios much higher than that and still not be in any danger of failing, but to produce top earnings most banks need to reduce their charge-off ratios.

To maintain a high performing bank, our goal for net charge offs to total loans should be from .15% to .25%. Any bank with a net charge-off ratio above .35% should probably institute a program of loan quality improvement.

The loan loss reserve should exceed total nonperforming loans. If it doesn't, our loan loss reserve account should be

increased. Other real estate as a percent of total assets
should be under .25%.

We could make an exception to these various credit
standards for those banks which have unusually large
credit card portfolios. We all know credit cards carry much
higher charge-off ratios than any other kind of bank loan.

Since most banks don't meet these standards, many
bankers will feel these goals are too stringent. We must
remember that we're talking about the characteristics of
high performing banks. We are not suggesting that banks
with higher charge-off ratios are in any particular trouble.

Nonetheless, if we can get past the initial arguments
over appropriate targets for various credit ratios, we can
examine the importance of loan quality in our banks.

After interest expense is deducted from interest income
to produce the net interest margin, the next item on our
income statement is a charge for the loan loss provision. If
our bank's loan portfolio is growing, we must immediately
increase this expense to maintain whatever level of loan
loss provision our management and board feels is appropriate. If, for example, our bank maintains a loan loss reserve equal to 1.25% of outstanding loans and our loan
portfolio grows by $100 million, we must put aside $1.25
million just to maintain our loan loss reserve level. That
transfer to the loan loss reserve comes out of current earnings. If our portfolio is not growing, we only need to put
enough in the loan loss reserve to cover new charge offs
less recoveries. Obviously, if we can maintain a high quality loan portfolio, our net interest margin after loan loss
provision will benefit.

CHARGE-OFF RATIOS

Unless the major earning asset in our bank is a huge charge
card portfolio, we'll want our annual charge-off ratio to be

somewhere under .35%. There are still a few banks around with charge-off ratios of five or 10 one hundredths of one percent. We'll never criticize high quality loans, but someone might ask such a bank if too many good loans are being turned down.

As a rule, bankers with high charge-off ratios will try to make a convincing case to justify their record. They will tell us that they are more interested in the community, more interested in helping the little guy, and more willing to take a chance. That may be perfectly true, but they're really not doing a favor for the borrower, his employees, his suppliers, or his community when they put a borrower in business even though he has very little chance of success. Many people besides the borrower and the bank are hurt by a business failure. The failed business results in people being put out of work, suppliers not being paid, the owner of the business property doesn't collect his rent, and the community doesn't collect taxes owed.

In any event, let's assume that we've decided that we would like to have a charge-off ratio of .30% in our bank. Let's also assume it's currently at .40%. What should we do? Maybe nothing. Charged-off loans are the exception; they represent very small numbers in relation to the total. If we have 10,000 loans in our bank, the difference between a charge-off rate of .30% and .40% is ten loans. Ten out of 10,000 is not a statistically significant number. The next year the same bank with the same officers and the same policies and procedures might produce .35%, .42%, or .49%; anything within a range of five or 10 basis points. While constant efforts to improve should represent the standard operating procedure, we must be careful not to make any drastic changes based on data that may be a blip on the chart and not the beginning of a trend.

If, on the other hand, we are faced with a charge-off ratio of .80% then we will want to get started on a loan quality improvement program. We should try to think of the loan division of our bank from two angles. First, we have the people involved: credit clerks, loan officers, collectors, and perhaps the loan workout people. Next, we have the "environmental system" of the loan division. This includes the credit department and its practices and procedures where statements are "spread" and analyzed, cash flows are plotted to ascertain that there is sufficient income to meet anticipated payments, credit history is investigated, and industry comparisons are made.

Next, we have the loan officer who is the bank's liaison with the customer. The loan officer's job is to bring the customer's needs and the bank's requirements together in a mutually beneficial arrangement. We have a loan committee that reviews, examines, and approves those larger loans that are over the lending authority of the individual officers. We have collectors who have responsibility for following up on and collecting past due payments. We have a loan work out person or persons who are involved when it's time to call the lawyers and sue, foreclose, or repossess whatever is available; and when necessary, to represent the bank in bankruptcy courts. We have operating procedures, loan policies, and a mission statement for the loan division of our bank. When these systems and relationships have not been materially changed in two or three years, they have reached a state of "equilibrium." Whatever charge-off rate this system is producing will continue pretty much unchanged.

When our charge-off ratio is too high, first we must try to determine if our problem lies with the people or with the system. Most bankers assume the loan officers are at fault, and they may be. But more often than not, the problem is in the system. It is possible to have a team of capable loan officers produce a consistently unsatisfactory charge-off ratio. This happens because the system, by its very design, produces a higher than satisfactory error rate.

People who have never been lenders often fail to realize that loan officers can't tell which borrowers will repay their loans and which won't. The officers think they can but they can't. Lenders only know that if they follow certain practices and policies, a sufficient number of borrowers will repay. Lenders can't accurately predict which specific borrowers won't pay; if they could, they wouldn't make those loans.

We can think of a fairly simple system involving residential home mortgages. Nationwide, if we include all borrowers and all lenders, among those mortgages carrying a down payment of 20% or more, there will be a foreclosure rate of 1.0%. This is not a loss rate, but a foreclosure rate. Of those mortgages with 10% equity, the foreclosure rate will be 1.5%. Of those mortgages with down payments of 5%, the foreclosure rate will be 2.5%.

Loan Approval Process

We have always known that the more the borrower uses his own money to invest in a home, the less likely the borrower is to walk away from his obligation. Most foreclosures occur in the third and fourth years of a mortgage. Beyond five years, the foreclosure rate declines dramatically. We also know that two, three, or four years into the mortgage, some of our customers will lose their jobs or their marriages will break up or some other major calamity will befall them. We can't predict which ones will suffer these hardships, but we do know that the ones with big equity positions will not let their homes be foreclosed on.

If our bank makes home mortgages with 5% down payments and we're experiencing foreclosures on these loans of 2.5% and we think that is unacceptable high, we shouldn't fire the loan officer. He's not the problem! The problem is in the system. If we want to reduce foreclosures, we have to stop making loans with 5% down payments. If we change loan officers, it will take three or four years to know if we have improved our position because it takes that long for most mortgages to go into foreclosure. If we increased our down payment requirements and kept the same officers, no matter what the foreclosure rate is now, it will be less in the future. What we need to change is our loan policy and that is part of the system. Most loans with 5% down payments will pay as agreed. If we insist on making such loans, we must do one of two things: accept the certainty of a slightly higher foreclosure rate or change another part of our loan policy. We might be able to offset the higher risk of small down payments by tightening other parts of our mortgage policy. This might mean lower qualifying ratios, no loans with "gift" down payments, no exceptions on credit requirements, and no exceptions on property qualities.

The whole loan approval process is simply a selection system. We know that for the most part, top-notch borrowers get their money from the bank down the street; they don't go five states away to arrange financing. If we lend money to borrowers outside our normal banking area, we have already adversely affected our selection process. We have eliminated the best borrowers from our sample. If our bank is in Atlanta and we are somehow put in touch with a borrower in St. Louis, we might conclude that people in St. Louis pay their loans the same as people in Atlanta. They probably do, but most of them don't go to Atlanta to arrange financing. If we take all of the borrowers in St. Louis who arranged loans out of state, we no longer have a normal cross section. We now have a group whose charge-off ratio is tremendously different from a normal sample. We have left out the best credit risks. If we routinely lend money outside our normal banking area, we will eventually experience loss ratios that are much higher than normal. The system will produce it no matter who is approving our loans. Even though these loans may seem to qualify on the same basis as our local borrowers, they are different in ways we cannot see.

The loan approval process is nothing more than a selection by which we try to weed out potential problems. We know that we lose less money on secured loans than on unsecured loans. We know that we lose less money if the borrower's income is two times the amount required rather than one times the amount required by our underwriting guidelines. We know a borrower has a better chance of success in an existing business than in a brand new business. We know someone who has defaulted on loans in the past is more likely to default in the future than someone who has always paid his or her debts on time. When we examine all of the above we are performing a selection process. Anytime our loan policy allows us to ignore a critical part of the selection process, we are increasing the eventual charge-off ratio our system will produce when stabilized.

We can think of the system as stabilized if we haven't materially changed it in two or three years. That means all of the procedures and policies have had time to have an impact on the quality of the portfolio, and the loans themselves have had time to get into trouble if they are going to.

Changing the System

Once the system is stabilized, whatever charge-off ratio it is producing should remain fairly constant within normal statistical deviations. As stated earlier, we can have a greater impact on the quality of our loan portfolio by changing the system than by changing officers. When we change the system, it affects all our loan officers at once and produces a much more pronounced and immediate effect.

A simple example of this might involve changing the policy on construction loans. Many banks have lost millions financing construction of various commercial real estate projects. Thirty years ago most banks required a 50% equity ratio on commercial mortgages and limited them to ten years. Over the years, the 10 years grew to 15 years, then 20, then 25, and now 30. The 50% equity requirement steadily shrank until now we find banks lending more than 100% of the real estate value in leveraged buy-out loans. Each time we reduce the equity requirement, we increase the charge-off ratio a little bit. Even though we know this, we find ourselves making even riskier loans for the reason that "everybody else is doing it." We have to meet the competition. When we hear bankers explain their actions by saying that they must meet the competition, we wonder if they have children. Every parent we know has at one time or another told their children, "I don't care if all the other kids are doing it, you're not! If they all jumped off a cliff, would you?" We must presume these bankers weren't paying attention when they received this admonition or if, when they use it themselves as parents, they think it only works for kids. Sometimes we sound a little like our kids.

What could banks have done to minimize losses on commercial real estate loans during the 1980s? The following three changes could have been made:

1. Require borrower equity investments of 20% or 25%.

2. Require reputable feasibility studies showing the project has a good chance of success.

3. Require a permanent financing take-out commitment to be in place that isn't riddled with loopholes.

Just those three changes to the system would have had a dramatic impact on charge offs. If other banks are making loans on more liberal terms, we should let them; they will have higher charge offs than our bank. If we expect to out-perform the competition, we can't do exactly the same things they are doing.

Reducing Charge Offs

To produce lower charge offs. The following steps should be taken:

1. We should review loan policy and make any changes deemed necessary, even if they are subtle changes.

2. We should make sure the policy is being followed and we should minimize exceptions.

3. We'll review credit write ups and make sure all pertinent information is routinely provided, including a cash flow analysis to be sure the ability to repay is demonstrated.

4. We'd make sure the officers' loan committee hasn't deteriorated into a "good old boy" club. It's easy for this to happen: "We won't ask any difficult questions about your loans if you don't ask any difficult questions about ours." If the loan committee has more than five or six members, the responsibility has been too thinly diluted. With 10 or 12 members on a loan committee, nobody is responsible. If we reduce the number of members, we can improve the quality of the decisions.

Many loan committees have a simple majority requirement for a loan approval. We once examined a bank where the loan committee had 13 members and 7 yes votes approved the loan. Even though six experienced lenders thought the loan shouldn't be made, if seven thought the loan was acceptable, it was approved. If we had a loan pool consisting solely of loans which had been approved by a 7 to 6 vote, what kind of charge-off ratio might we expect from such a pool? Less than one-half of one percent? Hardly.

A simple majority might be adequate when electing a president, but the results of such a system are unsatisfactory when approving loans. Two "no" votes should be sufficient to turn down a commercial loan request.

But suppose we suspect one or two or more of our loan officers are really unable to perform in a satisfactory manner? What should we do? First, compile a list of charge offs over the last year or two and see if one or two loan officers' names appear too frequently. We can't blame the loan committee for all the bad loans they have approved. The loan officer handling the account must accept most of the responsibility for the loan's quality. Assume the charge-off numbers of one loan officer prove to be more than the normal deviation that we might expect from chance selection. We should then examine the credit files of the charged-off loans of the officer in question to see if there were any warning indicators that were overlooked or ignored. If, when we've reviewed the files, it is obvious to us that the loans were bad decisions the day they were made, what should we do? There are several options, the first of which is fire the officer. This choice is quick, decisive, and final. Instead, we might reduce or eliminate the officer's loan limit until he has had further training and demonstrates to his superiors that he has improved his ability to evaluate credit. We could reassign him to a job that doesn't involve approving loans. The one choice that is not available is to do nothing and hope for improvement. It won't happen. Nor will it be adequate to tell the officer that we want him to do a better job approving loans. He thinks he is doing a good job now. Nobody intentionally makes bad loans. The officer, when faced with the statistics, will believe that he has been the victim of bad luck, bad business conditions, or something else totally beyond his control.

If we are new to a bank and want to obtain a quick view of the individual lending philosophies of the people in our loan division, we might try the following. Give each loan officer a list of all our loan officers and tell them, on a scale of one to ten (with one being the most conservative and ten the most liberal) to put a numerical score after each lender including themselves. Pick up the reports, add up the scores, average them out, and we'll have a remarkably accurate reading. We can run our bank with anybody carrying scores from two to seven. Since most scorers tend to cluster around the middle, anyone with an average score of eight, nine, or ten is widely recognized as being very liberal. Someone with this score will almost certainly have high or high average problem loans. They will usually be candidates for further education or reassignment.

Finally, most loan officers who have higher than average charge offs are not stupid. Some of them are technically very knowledgeable. They can discuss credit with anyone, but somehow they are unable to apply the knowledge when sitting across the desk from a real live borrower. They will believe anything if the person talking to them is sincere.

Often the problem is not that the loan request should have been declined. It's just that the loan officer neglected to obtain a lien on collateral that was available or doesn't insist on obtaining personal guarantees before funds are advanced. These little things make the difference between winning and losing when those unanticipated problems develop somewhere down the line.

In summary, if we want our charge-off ratio to improve, we should first check the delinquency ratios and charge-off ratios of our individual loan officers to be sure no one is off the charts. If we do have such a loan officer, we must re-place him immediately before he destroys the bank.

Review Loan Policies

The next step is to review all of the elements of our loan system. We should tighten up all of our policies and make sure everybody knows that they are to be followed. Such tightening might include larger equity requirements on real estate loans and elimination of "soft" costs when calculating real estate value. Soft costs might include expenses of land clearing, title insurance, legal fees, franchise fees, and anything else beyond the building itself.

We might increase our required "coverage ratio." A coverage ratio is the relationship between the debt payment and the amount of money available to make the payment. If we require a coverage ratio of 110% of the amount required to meet loan payments, this could be increased to 125% or calculated off a lower occupancy ratio. We can finance a slightly lower percentage of inventory or receivables. We might decide to finance only billed receivables less than 30 days delinquent. We can limit unsecured lending to a certain dollar amount. We should have a more stringent policy on very large loans. No bank can afford a charge off equal to its legal lending limit. If we don't have a lower "house" limit on loan size, we should at least try to get the risk level of these larger credits down to almost zero. It is possible to materially change the charge-off performance of a bank by simply loosening or tightening all of these variables. It is much easier, more effective, and more immediate than changing individual officers.

It seems that most banks have at least one or two lenders who shouldn't be making loans, but fortunately they usually don't get too high in the organization. When we find such people in our bank we should take corrective action immediately, but we should first be certain that the problem is the person and not the system.

Don't Set Volume Goals

Don't set volume goals for loans. Take what the market will give at the price and credit standards we find acceptable. We shouldn't try to force volume out of a market that doesn't have it. We've seen bankers try to increase loan volume and then become upset when margins shrink and charge offs rise. Why are they surprised? When they tell their commercial loan officers they must increase volume by 20%, what do they think those loan officers are going to do? Do they really believe that they need only call on their competitor's best customers to increase volume? Do they really believe the best borrowers are going to leave a bank with which they have enjoyed a good long-term relationship simply because someone shows up and asks them to? Our loan officers will offer the new prospects lower rates to get them away or they'll eliminate the need for personal guarantees or some other onerous credit requirement. Rates on the entire portfolio will then sink lower.

Anybody who has ever been a commercial loan officer knows how it works. A new car dealer's wholesale floor plan line is presented at prime plus one half. All of our other car dealers pay prime plus one on floor plan lines. The officer with the new account says, "I can get this business at prime plus one half. That's what he's paying now. He'll come to us for the same rate, but he won't pay more than he's paying now. Do we really want more business or don't we?" The loan is approved. Five other officers who handle car dealer floor plan lines are all too aware of the rate. Why should this new borrower, who doesn't even have an account here, get a better rate than our existing loyal customers? Why indeed? Besides, these dealers all talk to each other. What do we tell our long time customer when he finds out his competitor, who is brand new to our bank, is getting a better rate? The next time each of these other lines comes up for renewal, the rate will be prime plus one half. The officers will explain that we have to reduce the rate one-half percent or we'll lose the account. Besides, my customer is as good as yours.

The net result of all this is that rates on all wholesale lines have been reduced in order to get one new customer in the bank. It wasn't planned that way. Management really believes that we can bring in a new customer at a lower rate without affecting the pricing on our existing portfolio. It can't be done. The exact same thing happens when the new car dealer gets his wholesale line without providing a personal guarantee. The next time the lines are renewed, the other guarantees will be released; and any new dealers we sign up will be without a guarantee at prime plus one half.

It doesn't matter whether we're working with auto dealers, gas stations, liquor stores, clothing stores, or McDonald's. When we relax credit standards to get a borrower out of a competitor bank, all other borrowers like them eventually are given similar terms. It has nothing to do with banking or economics; it's psychology, it's sociology, and it's human relations. Loan officers are people first.

We shouldn't set volume goals. Although we must assume some volume numbers when putting together a profit plan, the amount of earnings wanted should be the goal, not the volume of loans.

When loan volume is down, so are interest rates. That's what happens in the trough of the business cycle. Instead of forcing loan growth, take the extra point income and capitalized service fees available from increased mortgage volume. There are other things happening in other parts of the bank in a low rate environment. We must take advantage of them. Deposit costs can decline faster than interest income because entire portfolios are immediately affected. We shouldn't try to drive the entire bank through the commercial loan portfolio. The result will be a relaxation of credit and pricing standards that never pays off in the long run. It's simple arithmetic.

CORRECTING BAD PORTFOLIOS

All of the above credit tightening measures can produce lower charge offs in the future, but they won't help much if we have a bad portfolio right now. If the quality of our current portfolio is unsatisfactory, we can do all of the above to stop adding fuel to the fire, then consider several other steps to deal with existing problem loans.

Once a loan is identified as being a serious problem, we should take it out of the hands of the original loan officer. He has too much of himself invested in the account. When the borrower comes in and says, "You have to give me another hundred thousand or I can't meet my payroll on Friday. I'll have to lock my doors and shut down the company," it's very difficult for the account officer to refrain from throwing good money after bad. The loan officer wants to "work it out." Millions of dollars are lost because many banks don't take problem loans away from the original loan officer quickly enough.

A professional "workout" officer is more concerned with protecting the bank's interest and collecting the money. If the borrower's business survives, fine, but at this stage of the proceedings, the bank's interest comes first. If we do not have a loan workout officer who knows his way through the bankruptcy courts, we will probably do better hiring an experienced person than trying to train one of our current officers. For one thing, there is nobody to train him, and trial and error takes too long and doesn't work very well.

The loan workout officer should report to someone higher than the people whose loans he's collecting.

Loan workout officers must be tough. They must put the concerns of the bank first. They must decide when to foreclose, when to repossess, and sometimes, when to put the borrower out of business. The loan officer has usually built up a personal relationship with the borrower. The loan officer would often be too slow in taking corrective or protective action. If he could, the loan officer would often hold off the collection process to the detriment of the bank's interests. Loan workout officers must feel free to take whatever action they believe is in the best interests of the bank without worrying about being overruled or receiving below average performance appraisals or salary increases in the future. There must be a separation of control between lenders and workout officers just a there is a separation of control between lenders and auditors.

If we are using our bank counsel to routinely collect bad loans, we might want to consider a law firm specializing in collections. Most lawyers don't like the work. They don't move fast enough, are too willing to compromise, and are not tough enough. We know there are exceptions, but most bank lawyers are too polite for collection work, particularly in a small community.

Review Collection Policy

We should also review our collection policy. Some banks don't send a first notice until 16 or 20 days after a payment is due. They may save some postage by giving chronically slow payers time to make payments without a notice. Unfortunately, some people cannot be allowed to get more than a few days past due or they'll never get back on track. Some of them can be saved by early action, particularly the new borrowers. The first notice should go out before the grace period has expired. A telephone call should follow immediately after the grace period. We can reduce the number of eventual charge offs with early attention. It will also reduce our delinquency rate.

When we foreclose on residential real estate, the lending officers usually try to sell the property at a price sufficient to pay off the balance on the loan, the lawyers, the fee, and anything else connected with the credit. And often, they don't like to send good money after bad. Nonetheless, it is usually best to spend some money on the property; paint it, clean it, and try to make it as presentable as possible. Offer the realtor a bonus if he can get a signed contract in 30 days; he may try a little harder. Finally, we should take the best realistic offer that we can get. Our interest income is suffering until we turn that real estate into an earning asset. We shouldn't wait an extra six months to get the last one thousand dollars out of the property to avoid a charge off.

When we know the loan is headed for foreclosure and before the borrower has left the property, it is often wise to take the following approach. Once a loan is recognized as a problem, the transfer to loan work out should automatically take place at some stipulated point.

If there is a common weakness in bank loan divisions, it concerns what happens between the time a loan is recognized as a problem and the time it is eventually charged off. Generally, things don't happen fast enough. A written policy could help. Nobody can collect money from a borrower who has no money. But faster, tougher action can reduce losses, particularly when the officers and lawyers involved are specialists.

Human nature being what it is, most bankers would like to find one or two officers or procedures to blame for a bad loan portfolio. It rarely works out that way. Dozens of small adjustments in policy and procedure are generally required and usually produce more immediate and more permanent results. Simply firing the head of the loan division or the loan officer with the worst record may be tempting and indeed necessary, but it won't have the widespread impact that changing policies and procedures will, and we won't know for three or four years if the new people are any better than the ones who have recently departed.

SUMMARY

A higher than average charge-off rate doesn't only produce a higher than average loan loss provision. It also requires more collectors and more loan workout officers. It reduces the yield on the loan portfolio because nonperforming loans yield zero. Other Real Estate Owned reduces the ration of earning assets to total assets, and increases several other categories of "other expense," such as insurance, real estate taxes, legal fees, and property management expense.

For all of the above reasons, it is absolutely critical to maintain a high quality loan portfolio. There simply are no high performing banks with a large percentage of problem loans. Loan charge offs must be kept to an absolute minimum and we must totally eliminate any idea that we can somehow make up for a higher charge-off ratio with greater volume.

7 NONINTEREST INCOME

Throughout the decade of the 1980s, although there were temporary ups and downs, interest rates generally drifted downward. Because most banks were liability sensitive during the early 1980s, this was not a problem, but that quickly changed. People refinanced mortgages in numbers never before witnessed, and some people refinanced several times. This accelerated the anticipated payments on mortgages to such a degree that many banks became asset sensitive and falling rates became a problem.

Then the tax changes in 1986 eliminated the tax deductibility of most consumer debt. Many people paid off credit cards and installment loans with second mortgages which had longer maturities and lower rates. These shifts on bank balance sheets caused interest margins to be compressed. To make matters worse, the collapse in the price of oil created immense economic and then real estate problems in every oil producing state. Banks then experienced substantial real estate loan losses. Bank regulators, not wanting to be accused of getting caught flat footed as they were in the southwest, made matters worse in New England where we saw the introduction of performing nonperforming loans.

Because of the cumulative negative pressures brought on by all of the above, banks turned to fee income to make up the shortfall. The late 1980s and early 1990s saw dramatic increases in all kinds of noninterest income. As a result, banks have recently developed more new dollars of revenue in the noninterest income area than in any other. As net interest margins became compressed from all of the factors already mentioned as well as the competition brought on by the deregulation of deposit rates, bankers looked for other sources of income.

If we compare our bank to others that produce much better ratios of noninterest income, we must be careful. Some banks have developed huge charge card portfolios that distort several statistics. Others have mortgage companies, trust companies, or discount brokerage companies. Even when these companies are unprofitable, they produce large amounts of noninterest income and can distort the various ratios that involve noninterest income. When we decide to embark on a program of earnings improvement from noninterest income, there are several approaches that we can take.

If, for any reason, we decide not to attack the issue in-house, we can always hire outside consultants to undertake the job. Some of them are really very good and worth every penny of what they charge. However, if we'd rather not take a chance on an unknown company, or would rather not spend money today in the expectation of a future pay back, there are still many things that we can do internally. The thing that makes a campaign to increase noninterest income so attractive is that the rewards are immediate. If we raise our service charges this month, our income goes up next month.

We can think of noninterest income as originating from two main sources. First, there is the typical array of service charges and fees assessed by the many departments of a bank. Next are fees coming from the nonbank subsidiaries. We'll begin by considering nonbank subsidiaries.

NONBANK SUBSIDIARIES

We should decide whether we want to start or purchase any new companies. If we don't already have a mortgage company, we can get into the business of originating, pooling, and selling residential mortgages on a relatively small scale without starting a new company. It is the most economical way to get our feet wet. If we pool, sell, and service some of our mortgage originations, even if we guess wrong about the direction of interest rates, we can simply keep the loans. If we have a separate mortgage company, these loans have to be "marked to market" each quarter. That means if rates rise and the market value of these mortgages fall, we have to take a charge to earnings. The most common mistake made by banks entering this business is trying to do it with the current mortgage manager. Hire an experienced mortgage banker. There are much more stringent documentation requirements in the secondary mortgage markets. A "white out" on a note causes it to be rejected. The mortgage pools must be constructed to produce an investment quality instrument. Underwriting standards are very detailed and specific as are appraisal standards. The average commercial bank mortgage officer can learn all these things, but it takes a long time and many costly mistakes occur during the learning process, especially since there is no teacher available. The business is much more complicated than most nonmortgage bankers realize, and it is anything but risk free. When mortgages are sold to Fannie Mae or Freddie Mac, the mortgage originator makes many warranties to the purchaser concerning credit quality, property quality, underwriting standards, and documentation. The bank's president may be told that "all is well" by the mortgage officer only to learn several years later that a subsequent audit has uncovered widespread failures to meet some secondary market standard. The bank may then be forced to buy back millions of dollars worth of loans which are in some way flawed. Nonetheless, the business can be very rewarding.

A word of caution: Don't expect a mortgage company to perform like a commercial bank. Mortgage companies turn over their inventory every two months. They can go from the joy of victory to the agony of defeat much faster than a bank. They are one-product companies dependent on the housing industry and the direction of interest rates. Running a mortgage company is a little like running a trading account.

When interest rates are falling, everybody in a mortgage company is a genius. We buy something today and sell it next week at a profit. We commit to a mortgage rate today and by the time the loan closes, rates have fallen and we sell it at a profit. The exact opposite is true in a rising rate environment. We must perform brilliantly just to break even. The loans can't close fast enough. If we try to hedge too far into the future, the cost of the hedge is so high that we lose money with it even when it works. The unhappy alternative is to price our loans out of the market.

Generally speaking, we lose money originating mortgages, even though the point and the fee income seems attractive. If we have a separate mortgage company, all overhead will be clearly identifiable. We will quickly find it is very difficult to turn a profit on originations. We should at least break even on the selling or marketing of the loans. The profit is in servicing pools of mortgages. It takes a few years to build up a servicing pool large enough to provide a good profit stream, but it really is worth the effort if we are not totally driven by next quarter's earnings. There are two major advantages of having a mortgage division capable of operating in the secondary markets. It allows banks to stay active in the residential mortgage business without overloading their balance sheets with long-term, fixed-rate assets. Secondly, when interest rates are falling and bank margins are being compressed, the mortgage division is at its peak. Mortgage company earnings are countercyclical to bank earnings. When rates are low the mortgage business flourishes.

If we do not now have a trust company or trust department, our advice is, forget it. Trust business takes a very long time to develop. A trust department might be named as executor on 10,000 wills, but they earn nothing until somebody dies. The most profitable kinds of trust business are already being done by highly skilled professionals. Trust activities carry substantial liabilities for mismanagement, and charges of mismanagement are often difficult to defend before an untrained jury. Because most fees collected by a trust department are dependent on the value of the assets under management, when the stock market falls, so does the income of the trust department. If we don't already offer these services, we will be well advised to study the matter very thoroughly before starting from scratch. It requires trained professionals, a lot of specialized handling, and a lot of patience. We shouldn't enter the trust business hoping to beef up earnings next year. Trust profits come over a long period of time. We might be better off using a correspondent bank to handle our trust needs.

Everything we said about trust departments goes double for discount brokerage companies. Discount brokerage is highly competitive, very price-driven and huge volumes of business are required to benefit from currently available technology. There seem to be a few nonbank affiliated discount brokerage firms that are able to control most of the market. If we are embarking on a program to increase noninterest income, there are better places to start.

Instead of starting a new company of some kind, there are always opportunities to improve noninterst income within the bank. We can eliminate waived fees, review all existing fees, with an eye toward raising as many as possible, and we can introduce new fees to start charging for things that used to be free.

STANDARD FEES

When we look at all the standard kinds of fees banks charge, there are very few, if any, that we can't simply increase today without losing many customers if the increase is not too severe. Many banks still offer free accounts to all kinds of customers.

If we have the nerve, we can institute charges on all of these. We will lose some accounts, but we'll also collect a lot of fee income. If we decide to institute charges for customers who have had free service (such as senior citizens), we can establish a minimum deposit requirement so they can avoid charges by maintaining sufficient balances.

COLLECTING CHARGES

We must make sure we are collecting charges for everything we reasonably can. When IRS attaches an account and ultimately claims the balance, we should deduct a fee for our services.

We shouldn't let doctors, lawyers, dentists, accountants, or insurance agents run businesses through a personal checking account. It's surprising how many do. We might want to review any personal accounts with more than 15 or 20 items deposited in a month to see if they really are personal accounts. We have seen "personal" accounts with hundreds of checks a month running through them for free because they stayed above the personal account minimum balance requirement. To add insult to injury, some of them were NOW accounts.

Bond coupon collection fees are often waived. Collecting coupons costs extra at the Federal Reserve Bank. We shouldn't do it without charging. If money market accounts drop below the minimum balance required, charge a fee. With credit card customers, charge a fee for anything and everything that is not routine such as returned checks, over lines, and lost cards.

We should charge a fee for returned deposited checks. If we automatically re-enter checks returned for a big volume check depositor, we should charge for it.

If a customer has payments of any kind set up to be automatically charged against his account, charge for it when these items are returned, the same as we would for a returned check.

Eliminate free accounts for estates, nonprofit organizations, religious organizations, senior citizens, lawyers directors, and friends. If we give free accounts to students, we must make sure our computer has some kind of "waive until" feature or the account will be free forever.

Charge a deposit fee for safe deposit keys and keep it if they are not returned. When drilling a box because of lost keys, add a profit to the actual drilling cost. We could raise all of our safe deposit fees and replace our smaller boxes with the more popular larger sizes. Charge more for boxes requiring a bill as opposed to those on which we simply charge the depositor's account.

Centralize all checkbook orders with one supplier and negotiate better service and a better price in return. This will allow us to make a profit on checkbooks and still have a competitive price for the customer.

Do not analyze "overdraft" or "not sufficient funds" charges against account balances. Use a direct charge and collect what is due.

This is not a comprehensive list by any means, but it is meant to highlight some of the routine ways banks can increase noninterest income.

Checking Account Service Charges

We once analyzed a bank with very low service charge income as a percent of demand deposits. First, we reviewed the bank's checking account service charge structure. It seemed appropriate. Then we discovered that over 50% of the bank's accounts paid no service charges at all because they carried "service charge waived" codes. This bank empowered all officers, including branch officers, to make any account exempt. As a result, anytime anyone complained about service charges, the officers simply made the account exempt. Add that to family, friends, and accounts lured away from other banks, and we eventually had more free accounts than paying accounts. The problem was solved when all "waive" codes were removed. Officers were told that the way to get "waive" codes reinstated was to write a memo to an executive vice president explaining why the account should be free. Very few customers left, and very few memos came in. Service charges on demand accounts approximately doubled in a single month.

We can very often improve income dramatically by simply reducing the amount of service charges waived. Waiving service charges can become a common practice without anyone even noticing. To check on this, we would obtain "waiver" reports, set goals for reducing the amount of waived fees, then follow up to be sure it is being done. If necessary, drastically reduce the number of people with authority to waive fees. In some banks we can increase income more by reducing waivers than by raising current fees or instituting new ones.

In addition to reducing the amount of service charges waived, it is also important to make sure tellers are collecting fees when they should be. Many banks want to charge noncustomers for cashing checks on other banks but their tellers routinely do not collect those charges.

One quick way to increase service charge income is to reduce the earnings rate on deposits in business accounts. It is immediate and it covers all such accounts.

Some banks charge more for paying an overdraft than they charge for returning a check. This makes sense. We are certainly providing our customer with a greater service when we cover his overdraft than when we return his check. Some of those overdrafts are not made good and a loss to the bank occurs. Some bankers don't realize how many dollars are involved with overdraft and return item fees.

Other banks have changed the order in which their computers pay checks. When a depositor's checks come in, if the computer pays the smallest amount first and progresses upward, the program minimizes the number of returns and minimizes the bad check fees collected. Those bankers probably feel they are doing a favor for their depositors, but perhaps they are not. If the order were reversed, and the largest checks are paid first, the number of returned checks would increase and so would returned check charges. Is this unfair to the customer? Maybe not. The largest checks most people write is their mortgage payment followed by their car payment. These are the last checks they want their bank to return. Most people would rather have their check to the supermarket or shoe repair store returned. They don't want checks bouncing that might damage their credit standing. We may not be giving them the best service by trying to minimize the fees paid.

If this sounds too avaricious, then we could establish "occurrence" caps. If, for example, the customer makes an error that would result in 10 returned checks in one day, instead of charging $20 each for a total of $200, the bank might establish a "cap" of $60. This would probably apply only to personal accounts.

Still another approach might be to pay checks in check number order. That way the bank posts the checks in the same order in which the depositor wrote them. The bank can hardly be faulted for doing that, and this approach produces more fee income than paying the smallest checks first.

Sometimes members of senior management focus most of their attention on loans and investments leaving bad check processing to junior officers. There is often a very large amount of income riding on simple decisions such as which checks to pay first and people in operations seldom consider themselves as income producers for the bank.

Some banks have increased the fees collected on traveler's checks from 1% to 2%. These fees haven't changed in decades, so maybe they are due for an increase.

On a cycled basis every single fee and charge the bank assesses should be reviewed annually. If this isn't done, we can find that certain charges we all take for granted haven't changed in 10 or 20 years. While we don't want to overdo it and risk killing the goose that lays the golden egg, we should still make sure that fee income grows on an annual basis.

Securities Profits

With the "held for sale" and "hold to maturity" classifications required in the investment portfolio, it has become much more difficult to actively manage a portfolio. Nonetheless, some banks still maintain considerable amounts in the "held for sale" portfolio, and some opportunities still exist to take securities gains. Although securities profits can sometimes be a lifesaver, some bankers rarely if ever take them. Some bank analysts treat securities gains as if they were in some way unclean. So do the bank regulators, most of whom don't really understand how to manage an investment portfolio. The perception seems to be that we are robbing next year's earnings in order to look good this year. That may sometimes be true, but it isn't always that way. At certain times it is possible to take securities profits without hurting the bank's annual income stream.

The simplest example involves "moving out the yield curve." Suppose current two-year treasuries yield 10%, three-year treasuries are 10.5%, and we have a treasury with a two-year maturity yielding 10.5%. We can sell the two-year treasury at a profit because it is yielding more than two-year issues and reinvest the proceeds at three years to yield the same 10.5%. If we had two-year treasuries yielding 10%, we could sell without a gain or loss and reinvest at 10.5%. Most bank analysts find nothing wrong with the second transaction whereby the yield of the portfolio is improved somewhat by lengthening it a little. However, they seem to have trouble with the first transaction, in which the same lengthening produces securities gains but no income increase. It's not clear why they feel differently in the second case.

Another opportunity exists when a treasury is slightly above water. We take the profits and reinvest them in an agency issue that yields about one-quarter percent more than treasuries. By going from treasury to agency issue, we can take security gains without giving up income or lengthening maturities.

If we have a two-year treasury yielding one percent under the yield curve, and a five-year treasury yielding one percent above the yield curve, we can sell them both and reinvest the proceeds at a yield halfway between them. The loss on the two-year issue will be less than the gain on the five-year issue because of the different maturities. The income stream hasn't changed, the average maturity is not changed materially (depending on the shape of the yield curve), and we have booked some securities profits. Unless interest rates are at recent highs or lows and have been there for some time, these kinds of swaps are almost always available. Because not all securities are as neatly arrayed as in the example above, it may be difficult to see this kind of trade by scanning a portfolio printout. Some securities are for one million, and others are for more or less. Some are a little under or above water, and some are a lot. They come in all different maturities, and they are not listed on computer printouts in any way that helps the officer to see these opportunities. If we have someone familiar with both Lotus and investments, they can develop a program to find these matches for us.

Additional income is sometimes available when two-yield curves are sloped differently. A few years ago, the treasury yield curve rose until it reached five years and then it was flat until it reached the end at 30 years. The municipal bond yield curve rose steadily to 15 years. That meant we could sell a treasury on the yield curve at 10 years, and a municipal bond on the yield curve at two years, then buy a municipal at 10 years and treasury at two years. We haven't changed our liquidity, average maturity, rate sensitivity, treasury to muni mix, or anything else. In effect we have swapped a low yielding treasury for a high-yielding muni. At one time, the difference was 350 basis points. A 10-million swap improved earnings $350,000 annually. (We know that doesn't produce a securities profit, it does increase interest income.)

With changes in the tax laws making munis less popular, many banks are switching to high yielding, mortgage-backed securities. Because munis are still tax free to individuals (at this writing), they are priced higher than they would be if they were being purchased by a bank. We can sometimes take a profit in munis, transfer to a mortgage-backed security, and not give up any income.

The swaps described above enable us to take security profits without giving up regular income. When conditions are right, we can do the opposite. It is often possible to improve our bank's income stream from the investment portfolio without sustaining a securities loss in the process.

A bank may have to periodically review its policies toward securities profits. Gains on securities sales are often thought of separately from noninterest income. Perhaps that's because such profits are not regularly available. Or maybe it's because most banks do not include securities profits in their budgets. Nonetheless, there seem to be times when it makes sense to take these profits. Just because we can't plan on them on a regular basis is no reason not to take such profits when they are available, if done prudently.

SUMMARY

The whole question of noninterest income is perplexing. Some banks charge for every single little thing they do. Others believe that providing a lot of little services without charge brings customers into the bank for more profitable services. We have never been in favor of providing some service at a loss in order to attract other business that may be profitable. Situations may exist where this makes sense, but we are generally opposed to the practice.

For years banks have provided all kinds of services at no charge. The public generally perceives such services to have no value (or else banks would charge for them). None of this makes sense. Bankers work hard to provide value that is not appreciated or paid for. Customers assume that we somehow make money on the free service. We may as well charge for it.

Some colleges that don't have financial problems raise tuition to make students believe they provide a really high quality education. If it costs more, then it must be better, right? Maybe not.

Those banks with the biggest charge card portfolios seem to charge the highest rates. How do they do that? Some provide a package of side benefits that go with card ownership. People who own these high fee cards are sometimes similar to people who buy prestige autos. They may think the high price says something about the owner.

If we have a piece of other real estate owned that hasn't sold for several months, sometimes we'll raise the price and that often results in a sale. It doesn't seem to make sense but sometimes it works. All this rambling about price probably confuses the basic question of whether or not to raise fees. Whenever fees are raised, some people will leave a bank on principle, and they'll pay the same fees somewhere else. There's not much we can do about that.

Finally, one senior officer must be made responsible for increasing noninterest income. That person should report at least quarterly to the president, chairman, board, executive committee, or senior management group on progress made. Who receives the report is not as important as the fact that progress is being monitored. The report should include a list of changes which will be made over the next 12 months, who will make the changes, when will the changes be made, how much additional income is expected, which changes were scheduled for last quarter, were they made, and what were the results. There is too much money at stake to let some of it fall between the cracks. As nonbank competitors take more of deposits and loans, bankers can expect continued pressure on margins. This will have to be offset by more noninterest income and tighter controls on overhead.

Most bankers realize that they will lose some customers anytime they increase fees. If we are fearful of raising service charges, we should remember this: once we have raised fees, new customers will continue to open accounts tomorrow and the day after. For them, there has been no change. The negative fallout from fee increases is temporary, but the earnings improvement is permanent.

8 Overhead Control

Over the next decade, as outside competition places additional pressure on margins, more and more emphasis will be placed on reducing overhead. We are already seeing a proliferation of articles and books on "re-engineering" the business. This means redesigning systems, procedures, policies and methods, hardware, and software; in short, it means starting over from scratch in deciding how we should be getting the work done. We approach this chapter with caution because we still believe the best route to superior earnings is by delivering outstanding service and charging a little more for it. Overhead reduction will be an ongoing concern in the years ahead because the bank with the lowest overhead will be able to price most aggressively or produce better earnings than its peers.

At the risk of overdoing the cost cutting and hurting service, we still must recognize that some banks do have overhead levels that are obviously out of line. Surprisingly, we have never found any correlation between banks with great service and high overhead. We don't need high overhead to deliver superior service. There is a difference between cutting costs and cutting corners.

If we can keep a realistic eye on service while reducing overhead, some savings are usually available. It's a question of balance. Almost every bank branch in America could operate with one more or one less teller. Adding a teller is no guarantee of better service if other shortcomings exist. It is also possible on many occasions to maintain good service with one or two fewer tellers.

Another word of caution. Bank holding companies with above average noninterest income generally also have above average overhead. This is to be expected. Overhead in banks is typically from 2.5% to 4.0% of total assets. Almost every other kind of business has overhead that equals a much higher percentage of total assets. It is not unusual for a mortgage company to service loans owned by outside investors that equal ten times their total assets. These loans are not on the mortgage company's balance sheet, but the overhead to service them is on their income expense report. Mix these numbers in with a bank's overhead, and the total produces a ratio that looks high for a bank or bank holding company.

If we think our overhead is too high, we must first be sure we're comparing apples with apples. We should separate the overhead of our banks from our nonbanks. We should do the same for noninterest income. If we have more nonbank subsidiaries than our peer group, we should expect more noninterest income and more noninterest expense than our peer group. Our overhead might seem high if it is compared on a total holding company basis. We could have a very efficiently run bank, and we might hurt the bank if we don't understand the impact on the ratios produced by the nonbanks. We must always be sure we are working on the right problem.

But let's assume that we've compared our bank with a fair peer group and they all have a lower overhead to total assets ratio. The numbers indicate that we need to reduce overhead. Where do we start?

If we are out of line with our peers, we must develop a plan to reduce overhead. We can take one of two approaches. We can put together an in-house campaign or we can hire outsiders to come in and do the job.

Outsiders are expensive, but some of them are well worth it. They also give us someone else to blame for some unpopular decisions. Some of these firms come in, interview our people, ask them what they do, how often they do it, and how long it takes. Then they count all the little transactions, multiply by each time factor, and determine how many man hours of work this constitutes. They then figure out when these things are happening and can build a chart showing how many people we need and when we need them.

These firms charge a lot of money and there are several basic shortcomings with their approach. First, they never ask "why" we put the pink copy with the blue copy, and whether we need to do it at all. Next, they accept our employee's estimate of how long it takes to put the pink copy with the blue copy. Third, the system requires hours of mindless ticket counting forevermore to maintain the program.

We once saw such a firm in action. When they were done, we discovered one branch seemed to require four times as long to underwrite a mortgage as another. We asked the firm whether one was doing the exact same things as the other. They weren't sure. Did they know if both or either of the numbers were accurate? They merely reported what they had been told. We asked if they knew whether the faster or slower number was correct. They did not know. Could they tell us what we should conclude from all this? They could not. What should we do with that data?

There are other firms that will come in and actually tell us which jobs to eliminate and which functions can be changed. If we are going to hire outsiders, we should question them very closely to determine exactly how they will proceed. If their success depends on our employees accurately telling them how long everything takes, forget it. Employees will not tell efficiency experts that they have a lot or even a little spare time on their hands. For that matter, neither will we.

When a firm gives us references, we should question their former clients closely. We can't simply ask, "Did they do a good job or did you get your money's worth from the firm?" Very few people who spend a million dollars on efficiency experts are going to answer, "No, we blew it. It was a total waste of money. We should have checked them out more." We must find out exactly what methods the firm used and ask ourselves if it all sounds right. Asking a person how long it takes to do his job and accepting the answer without question shouldn't cost much because the data isn't worth much.

We can reduce our staff more by announcing the following: "Next year we are bringing in efficiency experts. Their fee will depend on how many jobs they can eliminate. If you want to make points with the president, they better not find many dollars of savings in your division." By the end of the year your own people will probably reduce staff by 5% to 10%, and we'll be able to announce that in light of this outstanding accomplishment it won't be necessary to employ the professionals. If our numbers haven't changed, we can bring in the strike force.

REDUCING STAFF OVERHEAD

When we talk about reducing overhead, we're usually talking about body count. Salaries and benefits make up about one-half of total overhead. If we have too many people, then a whole group of other items of overhead are also out of line. Every one of those extra people has a chair, desk or work space, a telephone, a typewriter, computer terminal, or proof machine. These people create paperwork in personnel, use forms, and generally add to almost every other kind of overhead.

Too often, when banks decide to reduce staff, they concentrate on tellers, perhaps because there are so many of them and their function is understood by all. We may actually have too many tellers, but we'd rather start with non-customer contact people. Start by reducing staff in accounting, auditing, human resources, operations, credit, and the loan division and move on to the teller area later. One accountant can cost as much as five or six tellers. We should be careful when reducing staff in the customer contact areas, but we can't exclude them.

If a branch is staffed to comfortably handle the busiest time of the week, it will be overstaffed 80% of the time. That doesn't make good economic sense. People realize there are certain times when any business is busy. If we are trying our best, customers will usually accept a short wait.

Reducing Staff Yourself

Assuming we have decided to correct the problem ourselves, we can take any of several approaches, depending on the size of our bank. In a smaller bank we can simply walk around and get a good feel for who's always busy and who isn't. There are usually some kinds of transaction counts available from our branches. Perhaps 200 transactions per teller per day would be a reasonable base to start from. If the nature of our bank or systems seems to demand more or less, then a different base may be required. Simply comparing transactions per teller per branch will give us a good start. We'll usually discover surprising differences among our branches.

We might also simply institute a formal program whereby everyone in the bank is divided among several senior staff members who have responsibility for their areas. A count is taken at the beginning of the year. For one year each senior staff member will try to reduce the full-time equivalents under his or her control. At the end of the year, they will be paid a bonus of one thousand dollars for each job permanently eliminated. The staff must stay reduced for one more year. Half the bonus amount will be paid at the end of the first year. If the numbers stay down throughout the second year, the second half of the bonus is paid. Work that is contracted out doesn't count. This is not a perfect system, but one that will work and lends itself to easy scorekeeping.

The danger here is that staff will be reduced too much or that overzealous executives will eliminate faithful long-time employees in the pursuit of a bonus. Some other ground rules would have to accompany this program to protect the level of corporate morality. We do owe something to an employee who has been with us for 20 years or more and has always performed satisfactorily. We have to protect the loyal long-time employee from a random bloodbath.

If we are unfeeling, unfair, and callous in reducing staff, we will ultimately pay for it in the long run. We will lose the loyalty of those employees left. Some of them will leave and seek employment elsewhere. All of them will treat customers with a little less courtesy and caring. Most of them will eventually demand a little more pay because job insecurity demands a premium paycheck. People don't mind accepting a somewhat lower paycheck if they have job security.

We generally oppose those 10% across-the-board approaches. Invariably some areas shouldn't be cut at all, and in some, 10% is not enough.

When reducing staff, it is usually possible to do it through attrition. There is a high enough turnover in the work force to accomplish cuts at lower levels without actually letting someone go. At higher levels it is more difficult. The person has been with us longer. We'll want to keep the good ones, and the bad ones can't find work elsewhere. Early retirement plans can help. Lateral moves or out-and-out demotions may be necessary. It's never easy but inaction over time can build a very bad situation. Overstaffing breeds more overstaffing.

Judging from the age of our current population, we will be forced to become more efficient in banking, because the number of entry level workers will be declining in the 1990s and beyond. We presume this means we will have to use many more ATMs.

Nobody likes the idea of eliminating jobs, but most people understand it is difficult to continue to improve pay levels if we have too many people. If we pay all entry-level workers something near the minimum wage, we are missing some very good potential employees. Some good people will never come to work for us while others will come, get trained, and leave. Until banks figure out how to sort out the good ones and give them pay increases three or four times greater than the others, they will always be faced with high turnover, high training costs, and many marginally competent workers. We shouldn't try to reduce overhead by always hiring the person willing to work for the lowest paycheck. The best people cost more, but they are really worth it if we use them right.

A staff reduction program should be introduced in the right way. We're not doing it because we want everybody to work harder or because we think that employees are goofing off. We want them to work smarter, not harder. We should tell our employees that if they are doing mindless, unnecessary, time-filling tasks, tell us about them; we'll try to eliminate the junk part of the job so they can get it done easier.

We once walked into a 12-employee branch office and told the staff that we thought they could still provide good service with four fewer employees. It would involve scheduling lunch differently, eliminating a few practices such as getting holds on all checks, and coming in a little earlier some mornings so all night deposit bags could be done before opening. Then the employees were asked, "Do you think we can do that?" They said, "No." We said, "All right. Let us ask you another question. There are 12 of you here. Suppose we say, starting tomorrow, we will run this office with six people. Those six people will be expected to keep all of our customers happy and we'll pay them double their present salaries. The others will be transferred to other branches. Can we get six volunteers?" We got 12 volunteers. So some place between six and 12 was the right number.

If staff reductions can be coupled with simultaneous paperwork reduction and the elimination of unnecessary reports and approvals, then we will have a better chance to convince our people that we aren't just trying to make them all work harder. We really don't want our people going home exhausted every night. It shows in their customer contact behavior and burns them out. Nobody benefits.

If we can make work easier by adding equipment, we should do it. Our people have to believe that we are not simply taking advantage of them. We have to show them that we are really interested in making it easier for them to get the work done. Then we can get staff numbers down without turning our bank into an angry camp.

If all else fails and nobody wants to cooperate or be constructive about staff reductions, and our senior staff is more interested in preserving their turf than attacking overhead, then we'll go to plan B. We'll freeze all hiring until further notice and tell our officers that they will be expected to make do. They will be told to move people to where they are most needed, and maintain service until the numbers get down to where we think they should be. This is not really the best way to go about reducing staff, and we hesitate to recommend it, but we do believe that it is much better than doing nothing at all.

REDUCING OTHER OVERHEAD ITEMS

Aside from staff reductions, there are other items of overhead where we can save. How we go about it will depend on the size of our bank and the talent available to us.

In a small bank, we can gather two or three intelligent junior officers and put them on a special projects team for six months or a year. Their job will be to systematically review every category of overhead and report straight back to the president. We'll be astonished at what they'll find.

They might start by getting a list of every single subscription to every magazine and newspaper our bank is paying for. We'll find people in personnel receiving the *Wall Street Journal* and other people receiving *Newsweek*. We'll find a branch manager's home newspaper being paid by the bank. Should the president of the bank have to keep track of these things? Of course not, but when word gets out that the president cancelled a whole list of subscriptions, everybody will immediately begin to reexamine all overhead items. Nothing will be safe.

Count telephones and buttons and lines. Eliminate direct lines to branches. If we can't eliminate at least some, we're not trying. Install voice mail wherever it makes sense.

Insurance, Real Estate, Purchasing Practices

Bankers do some inconsistent things with insurance. We've seen banks with a million-dollar deductible on their blanket bond policy and a 200-dollar deductible on collision insurance on courier's vehicles. Insurance should protect us against calamity. It should protect us from a loss we can't afford to absorb.

It's pointless to pay extra premium dollars in the expectation of covering the first few hundred dollars of a loss that may never occur. We should raise deductibles on almost every kind of coverage and concentrate on reducing premiums. It might be wise to invite three or four major insurance suppliers to bid on all of the bank's insurance. We should ask for recommendations on how to reduce premiums without accepting risks above a certain specified amount. This will take a lot of time and effort and can't be done every year, but every four or five years it is worth a lot of money to any bank. Above all, we shouldn't put a little insurance coverage in every insurance agency that has a checking account with our bank. We will be wasting thousands and thousands of premium dollars and we will never be sure that we have everything covered because our insurance coverage is spread all over the place.

We should review the assessment of every piece of real estate the bank owns. We can then determine if any are obviously over assessed and try to get them all reduced. Some banks simply ask to have all assessments reduced.

Review purchasing practices. Our purchasing agent once told us he was about to order a year's supply of checking account statements. Before he placed the order, he wanted to know if we planned any change in the form. We said "no" but we asked if he was putting the order out to bid. We were buying hundreds of thousands of these forms. He told us Company A had always given us good service so he never bothered putting it out to bid. We told him to bid it. He said the prices wouldn't change. We had been paying $32.10 per thousand to Company A. When it went out to bid, Company A came in at $20.70. Company B came in at $19.50 and told us that they could reduce the price still further if we would accept a slightly lighter paper.

We don't have to put everything out to bid, and we don't even have to bid the big ticket items every year. Generally, good service from a supplier may even be worth a higher price. But on some high volume items in which quality is fairly standard, we ought to put them out to bid every so often just to keep everybody honest. If we're not going out to bid at least some of the time, the amount we will overpay for computer paper and other high volume purchases will be truly astounding. We generally don't approve of buying everything from the lowest bidder because, over time, the quality of items purchased may suffer. The exception involves certain high volume items of standard quality. Even here, there may be extenuating circumstances. If one firm holds a year's inventory, and delivers and bills as needed, it may be worth a few dollars more. We should also periodically bid the bank's annual fuel oil supply and contract cleaning. Accounting work can also be put out to bid but here, we should guarantee the winning firm that they will have the job for four or five years. An accounting firm must do much more checking the first year they have a new client. After that, they only need to update last year's numbers. If they aren't sure they will have the job more than one year, they will bid much higher than they will if they know they'll have the business for several subsequent years. Going out to bid periodically keeps most suppliers honest, but we should consider other factors as well.

With some computer systems we can save large amounts of money by simply printing eight lines to the inch instead of six. Six is a little easier to read, but most of what computers print never gets read anyway.

Computer Programming and Equipment Maintenance Costs

Most banks spend hundreds of thousands of dollars on computer programming because of changes made in the

standard software package. A junior officer prefers the borrower's name before the branch name or vice versa. Insig-
nificant changes like this cost big dollars, are never ending,
and are almost undetectable on the income statements.
Changes in the software should not be allowed without
approval from the highest levels of authority. Otherwise,
officers throughout the organization will incessantly order
changes that seem important to them, but which are not
worth the cost of changing programs.

A much bigger problem occurs when other improvements to the basic program are supplied by the producer of
the software and they cannot be readily installed. Once the
basic package is changed, future improvements must also
be changed so they will accommodate previous changes.
This is very expensive and often causes computer problems
no one ever anticipated. We should insist that basic software packages are not modified. If we want to sort delinquent loans by county or branch or hair color, we should
download data from the original system and manipulate
the data on a sub-system.

Equipment maintenance contracts were designed and
priced by suppliers of maintenance, not by users of equipment. Whenever practical, we shouldn't buy them. Sometimes, especially with copy equipment, they are almost un-
avoidable. For the most part, however, it will be cheaper to
pay for maintenance as needed. If our bank routinely buys
maintenance contracts, a thorough review is in order. Premiums on this type of insurance far outweigh the cost of
service provided.

Expense Accounts

Expense accounts really need close watching, partly because it's so easy to pad them and partly because it's so
easy to abuse them. Auditors should check restaurant tabs

with the restaurants (they keep originals). They should see if the numbered receipts match the restaurant's amount. Sometimes employees use tabs from restaurants that don't give tabs. They simply buy a pack of receipts and make out their own. If our people know we check such things, the expenses stay in line much better. We will also discover some officers seem to use the expense accounts five to 10 times more often than the norm. It may be perfectly legitimate, but they can spend much more on entertaining than makes any economic sense. Some standards are needed; not overly tight standards, but some standards.

All expense vouchers should be approved by a person's superior. No one should approve his own and co-workers should not approve each other's. If there are no controls, money will leak away. It becomes part of the corporate culture. On the other hand, if someone is fired for overcharging $10.00, a very specific message is sent out. Our bank doesn't tolerate dishonesty, not even a little!

Not only should all vouchers require a superior's approval, those over a certain specified amount should require a higher approval. No overnight travel should be allowed without some higher approval. Some people do an amazing amount of travel at the company's expense. Some seem to be able to find seminars to attend in a warm climate on a regular basis. These things can get out of hand without a system of internal controls to monitor such activity. We can also reduce travel and entertainment expense by requiring approval from our boss's boss. Most bank officers will routinely approve expense vouchers from people who work directly for them without much cross-examination. It's important to maintain good relations. But their boss's boss is not so close and will be less likely to overlook exceptions in the name of harmony.

If management wants to send a message that it is really serious about reducing overhead, they can eliminate company cars and country club memberships. If the troops will be expected to sacrifice, then senior management should demonstrate that they too are prepared to give something up. They might also reduce attendance at conventions.

All charitable contributions should be centralized to see that there is no duplication and that a sense of balance is maintained.

While management believes every report is necessary, all internal reports should receive a hard review at least annually to determine that the reason for the report still exists. It may also be possible to reduce the frequency of the report, or reduce the number of people who receive it.

Many banks are installing "voice response" units. These telephone answering systems can save the cost of telephone operators, but they can also be exasperating if they are too complicated or require too many opportunities to push the wrong button and make a mistake that can't be corrected without a call back.

All branches should periodically be reviewed for possible closing or consolidation with other branches. In the future, bank branches may be like gas stations of the past. We clearly have more than we need. What other industry constructs a million-dollar building to house five workers for five hours a day? Banks will eventually be forced to do better.

We can also introduce management bonuses big enough to produce results, reduce the number of board and advisory board meetings, use more part-time employees, reexamine the bank's fringe benefit package, reduce duplicate forms, review courier runs to see if they still make sense, reduce or eliminate the use of overnight mail service, establish travel and entertainment policy limits, and try to do everything faster. There is virtually no limit to the number of things we can do to reduce overhead if we insist on running a tight ship.

It is very important to develop a cost-conscious corporate culture. A bank that lets everyone know it is watching expenses (all expenses) will develop better habits over time. Everyone will learn to use intelligent cost/benefit considerations in all matters. Banks with inordinately high overhead are not run by imbeciles. There isn't much difference between them and the banks with better than average overhead. They don't have faster computers or geniuses on the teller lines. They just pay attention to a thousand details, they take cost control seriously, and they let everybody know it.

REDUCING OVERHEAD BY INCREASING PRODUCTIVITY

All of these are standard cost savers available to anybody who wants to take time to investigate. However, the best way to reduce overhead is to increase productivity across the board. This is a good deal more difficult to accomplish than increasing deductibles on insurance or cancelling some maintenance contracts.

Increasing productivity does not involve working harder or longer. It does not require frequent performance appraisals or establishment of goals and objectives. We improve productivity primarily by reducing errors. It takes many times longer to fix an error than it does to do the job right in the first place.

Think how many man hours of work we could save if nobody ever made a mistake. Most branch managers will tell you they spend over half of their time fixing mistakes made by others. Think of the hours and hours of research done everyday to track down errors and to correct them.

Most managers place the blame on poor work habits, and even those don't seldom place the blame where it belongs. Most bankers don't fully understand the high error problem, so they often work very hard to accomplish something that doesn't solve the problem.

Improving Teller Accuracy

Let's start with a fairly simple problem, teller accuracy. If a teller makes no mistakes during the day and runs all of the work correctly at the end of the day, he or she will "prove." If we have 100 tellers who have had between zero and 12 differences this month, what do we know? Perhaps we have calculated the average is six. An optimist might discover that half of our tellers are above average while a pessimist might decide that half of our tellers are below average. Should we focus our energies on improving those below average? No. The law of averages will place a truly "average" teller above average on half the measurements and below average on the other half. If the same teller consistently finishes in the lower half six months in a row, now what should we do? Perhaps that level of performance is the result of something besides teller competence. Perhaps that teller handles twice as many transactions.

The problem here is that teller differences are easy to· measure so we tend to measure them. However, it is extremely difficult to correctly interpret the data. Statistics can be misleading. We could spend a career trying to move tellers from the bottom half of performance into the top half, but no matter how hard we worked, there would still be a bottom half. We would go around in circles for several years without changing the total much. Clearly, what we must do is improve everybody's performance so we can get the average down. We should have the idea of always improving the performance of everybody as a never-ending goal.

Along the way, we must be extremely careful how we measure performance. If we measure tellers by production only, accuracy and friendliness may disappear while the teller whizzes through one customer after another. If accuracy is the only number we measure, the teller may slow down to a crawl while he triple checks everything. We may not really want absolute accuracy at any cost. And if the teller makes few mistakes, handles a good volume of work, and irritates every customer, we've still got a problem. Well, what exactly do we want?

We'd like every customer to feel wanted and appreciated, while the teller handles as many transactions as possible without making more than one or two mistakes a month. Maybe we'd prefer zero mistakes each month. While we'd really like to see zero mistakes, we may believe that it could cost more to achieve than it is worth, especially when we're first starting out. How do we get our employees to accomplish this? Do posters, slogans, goals, incentives, bonuses, prizes, contests, awards, rewards, or threat of firing work? No, none of these will work.

If we have a normal group of tellers who produce on average six errors per month, month after month, then what we have is a teller system designed to produce six errors per month. As long as we don't change the system, we'll continue to produce this error rate. Even if we replaced all of our tellers, it's highly unlikely that the new batch would be materially different from the old batch. On average, they would produce the same results. If we want to improve on the six errors per month average, we have to do something to change the system. To accomplish this, we have to talk to the tellers. We have to find out from them just what they need to reduce errors further. Maybe they need more adding machines. Maybe they don't have time to verify cash that is given to them. Maybe their cash isn't secure when they are away from the window. Maybe there's too much distracting background noise. Maybe a courier picks up their work before they can check it over.

Maybe they are asked to cover a window while they are opening mail deposits. Maybe the lighting is poor. Maybe the customer who claims to have been shortchanged is always assumed to be right. Maybe the teller doubles as a telephone operator. Maybe certain forms are difficult to read and or fill out. Maybe the teller has too many different kinds of transactions. Maybe the form of money orders or cashier's checks is confusing. Maybe other branch employees routinely interrupt tellers in the middle of transactions. Maybe the teller needs further training. Maybe all of the above and then some.

The Systems Approach to Improve Productivity

Is there a bank out there someplace that seriously attacks the work environment in the detail described above to help the teller do his or her job better? Do banks simply announce some new slogan and tell their people they "must do better"?

That kind of advice is useless. It's a little like your mother telling you not to catch cold. It's all well and good to establish goals and to set standards of performance, but how do we get everybody beyond those goals once they've been chiseled in stone? In the above example, suppose we announce that we want everybody to have six or fewer differences per month. A system designed to produce three differences will produce over six for several tellers every month. Are we to castigate that random group or try to get them all to improve still further? Besides, what will we do in the month everybody is at six or better? Accept that error level as the minimum achievable or continue to try to improve?

It's obviously important here that we don't convey the idea that we're never going to be satisfied. It must be the teller's desire to constantly improve his or her own performance, and he or she will do so as long as they recognize that we are trying to improve the system and the work environment.

This systems approach to improvement is necessary in every area and every level of the bank. If we are unhappy with loan charge-off levels, what will we do about it besides complain?

If we look at a simple product, the home mortgage, we find an interesting example. When "qualifying" a borrower for a loan, the underwriter uses two ratios. Assume they are 28% and 36%. Underwriters multiply gross monthly income by 36%, and from that number, they subtract all other monthly payments. That equals X. Then they multiply gross monthly income by 28% and that equals Y. Whichever is less, X or Y, is the amount of money available for a monthly payment of principal, interest, taxes, and insurance. If we want to reduce delinquencies and foreclosures, instead of hiring a new mortgage officer, we need only reduce the underwriting ratios of 28% and 36% to something less. The problem may be with the "system," not the people. A new officer will generally produce the same delinquency ratio using the same system.

If we're unhappy with our delinquency and foreclosure rate, it is much better to revise our policy, procedures, underwriting guidelines, and application source than to simply demand better performance from our mortgage officers. Unless they possess supernatural powers, an average batch of loan officers will give us whatever quality level our systems are designed to produce.

Most banks we've seen that introduce a "quality control" program start out by counting errors, circulating the information, printing a few posters, and waiting to see what happens.

Counting errors is not quality control; the mistake has already been made. Counting it doesn't change anything.

Something has to happen before the mistake is made. Circulating the bad news embarrasses the people involved; it doesn't motivate them. Employees resent posters telling them to "Do it right the first time," because it assumes they aren't already trying to do it right the first time (and I'm embarrassed to say I've used such posters). Most bankers would love to see productivity improve in their banks, but very few know how to make it happen. Instead, bankers do what bankers do best, they count things. They count errors, they count rejects, they count delinquents, they count charge offs, and someplace along the way they read something about management by objectives and they set a few. They want 10% fewer errors, 20% fewer rejects, 30% fewer delinquent loans, and 40% fewer charge offs. Then they sit back and wait for the results. Some of these numbers, because of normal statistical deviations, will blip in the right direction and the banker will feel gratified; and other numbers will blip in the wrong direction, so the bankers redouble their efforts and print some more posters. However, they have not yet treated the source of the problem.

The only bank that I've ever seen with a really good quality enhancement program is a money center bank with a relatively small consumer base. Even this bank was surprised at the extent of overhead reduction because that was not its primary purpose when the program was introduced. They were just trying to reduce errors and improve service. The reduction in overhead was a welcome but unanticipated surprise. We are convinced such a program is by far the best way to reduce overhead. This bank concentrated its quality program on back room operations where errors are easier to measure.

Later on the bank developed a program that tried to measure service quality in their branches. This included a monthly report card on each branch. Branches were shopped, telephoned, and inspected by customers in a way that allocated points to various aspects that were fairly easily measured. Some of the questions used include the following: When a branch is called by a customer, how often does the phone ring? Can the person who answered the phone answer the question? Is the information supplied accurate? Is the general tone or ambiance of the conversation satisfactory? This seemed to be working well but it involved a bank that had mainly very large branches. A smaller bank might find the cost to be too large, but some kind of measurement program will produce positive results.

The Public's Perception of Service

Even though it is difficult to measure service quality in a bank, it is possible to measure the public's perception of that service. We can survey the public by phone or mail to learn how they perceive our service. These results can be quantified and the survey can be repeated quarterly or semi-annually.

If such a survey is employed, everyone should know about it in advance. The whole program should be presented in a positive way. We are not trying to find out who is doing things wrong. We are trying to find out how we can serve our customers better. We want to be recognized as the best provider of bank service in our marketplace. This program is designed to help us achieve that goal. When the surveys are done, the results should be shared with everyone in the bank, even if the findings are sometimes less than flattering. We can't solve a problem if we won't recognize it exists. Most people want to do a good job, but they don't always realize how they are perceived by others.

Any service improvement program will have to include the reduction of errors. This is also where the overhead reduction will originate. The system must be worked on with tellers and supervisors, loan officers and their bosses, branch managers, and regional vice presidents. All of these people working together should continually reexamine the system to try to further reduce errors. They should monitor results together.

We can do more to improve productivity and reduce overhead by continually reviewing and improving our systems and work environments than we can by constantly exhorting our employees to "do better." If we can't tell them and teach them precisely what it is we want them to do differently, then we can't expect tellers to figure it out for themselves. They can help us with the methods if we can define our goals clearly enough.

Prior to attacking overhead, we should first determine the size of our problem. If we are more than 50 basis points above our peer group average, then we have a big problem, and we should employ every means at our disposal. If our bank is only five or 10 basis points off the average, then we might want to concentrate on a quality improvement program. We can reduce overhead to acceptable levels and improve service at the same time. If our overhead ratio is already better than average, the quality improvement program will be an added bonus.

SUMMARY

In summation, every bank can benefit from installation of a quality improvement program. More drastic action may be taken if necessary. If not, the development of a "cost conscious culture" should be sufficient to keep overhead in line.

Reducing overhead, like just about everything in banking, cannot be accomplished by a single action. Those banks that produce overhead numbers that are much below average do so by taking the time and making the effort to check on a thousand small things on a regular basis.

They check everything, they take nothing for granted, they attack every expense, and they let everyone know that waste simply won't be tolerated. They don't have any secrets or magic systems; they just work hard to produce a cost conscious culture and they persistently keep at it.

The business buzzword of the next decade, re-engineering, will be heard more and more frequently in our banks. Banks will try to reduce the number of layers of management, to re-examine the branch delivery system, to employ credit scoring in all areas of lending to reduce training time and empower more junior employees, and they'll try to computerize just about everything to speed things up and reduce errors.

Banks will have to accept change at heretofore unheard of levels, just to stay even with the competition. Overhead reduction is absolutely essential if the banking industry is to survive as a major player in the financial services business.

Finally, one senior officer should be designated as responsible for the bank's overhead reduction plan. He or she should report to the senior management group at least quarterly stating what will be done over the next 12 months, exactly when it will be done, and by whom. They will also report on what has been done, what didn't get done on time, why it didn't get done, and when it will get done—if ever. It's not enough to approve a plan; management must closely monitor its progress and make adjustments when necessary.

Over the next decade, there will be more changes in the way banks deliver their products than at any other time in history. Overhead levels will be cut in half. If we and our banks hope to survive, this is not the time to stubbornly resist all the changes that will seem to overwhelm us. Successful overhead reduction will separate the winners from the losers during the next five years.

9 OUTSTANDING SERVICE

Providing a level of service that is noticeably better than our competitors is the key to successfully paying a little less and charging a little more. If our customers are totally satisfied with the service they receive, if they are happy about the way they are treated, if they have positive feelings toward our bank and its employees, then they are receiving something of value that is hard to define and measure. It's worth something to customers to feel comfortable with their bank. Being absolutely sure your bankers will do everything that they can to help you when you need them, and being sure that they will know how to help you, gives customers a certain peace of mind that can't be measured in dollars and cents. Most customers who have this feeling won't leave our bank for one-quarter or one-half of a percent. How do we accomplish this? Where do we begin the process of building this level of service in our bank?

SET HIGH STANDARDS

We must set high standards at the very beginning. We should start out with a simple one sentence statement of what we wish to accomplish—and this has nothing to do

with earnings. Here we return to the original purpose of
banking and the fact that high quality is worth something
extra. If we provide that something extra, superior earnings
can follow. Perhaps we should begin by developing a single
sentence that clearly states what we will try to accomplish
with our service level. A starting point might be, "We want to
provide better service than any other bank in Arizona." We
might also consider, "We want our service to be noticeably
better than that of any other bank in Nebraska." We like that
better than the first statement because it is a little more specific. Maybe we want to have the friendliest bankers in our
state or maybe the most professional. We'll take friendly over
professional everywhere but New York City.

We should choose a single sentence so every employee
in our bank knows exactly what our intentions are in the
area of customer service. We must tell everyone in the
bank, and we should repeat it often. Then every decision
can be measured against the statement we adopt. Will the
action help or hurt our overall goal? Is it the kind of thing
the bank with the best service in Nebraska would do?

Spell out your goals. We must spell out our goals and put
them in writing. These must be specific and they can cover
everything from customer waiting time in teller lines to the
time it takes to approve a loan, correct a mistake, or return a
phone call. We must tell everybody what's expected and we
can't assume that it's common sense to do these things. Very
few people have common sense that is identical to ours.

Expect a lot—give a lot. We should expect a lot from our
employees, but we must also give them a lot. We should
help our employees get ahead. We demand respect for the
lowliest employee, especially from our officers and supervisors. Good customer relations begins with good employee relations. Every single employee is important. If we
don't believe that, we can try running a bank with a crew
of incompetent janitors. Respect for the individual is criti-

cal. If we expect our employees to treat our customers with respect, then we must treat the employees with respect. Officers shouldn't have preferred parking or any other special treatment. We shouldn't ever expect our employees to do anything or to tolerate anything that we don't do or tolerate ourselves.

We should demand outstanding performance for promotion. We never promote on the basis of seniority alone. Seniority can be the determining factor only when all else is equal, and all else is almost never equal. Nothing destroys morale faster than promoting unqualified people. If we don't have anyone in-house capable of doing the job the way we want it done, it indicates we have not done a satisfactory job of hiring and training the people we have. Our employees don't like to see people come in from the outside, but hiring a qualified outsider is better than promoting an unqualified insider. Sometimes there is no real professional on our bank's payroll who can train subordinates. The only way to take the bank to a new level of professionalism is to hire someone from outside. We shouldn't hesitate to do this when necessary, but we must be extra careful to insure the outsider is indeed an improvement over anyone currently employed.

Don't accept mediocrity. We can't accept mediocrity, not from anyone, and not at any time. There is no room for mediocrity anywhere in a high performing bank. If we have grumpy tellers, we can't let it go uncorrected. If we have a slow teller, we can't accept it. If we have five tellers handling two hundred transactions a day each, and one is replaced by a slower teller, a strange thing will happen. After a week or two the tellers on either side of the slow teller will slow down themselves. Then the others will also. Service will slow down, and before long we'll have to add another teller. A teller won't perform at full speed if the one alongside is a goof-off. One bad teller can ruin a whole branch. We can't accept it.

First, someone should talk with the poor performer and spell out exactly what's wrong, what's expected, and when it's expected. The poor performer is then told a follow-up meeting will be held in 30 days to determine if perform- ance has sufficiently improved. If the employee volunteers that some kind of additional help or training is needed, then it should be provided. One month later an updated performance review is completed, and another meeting will take place. If all is not well, one last chance may be given. The employee is told at this point that if perform- ance hasn't reached satisfactory levels in 30 days, then there will be no alternative but termination. Finally, we must do it.

JOB PERFORMANCE AND JOB SECURITY

For too long, too many people have felt that a job in a bank carries tenure. Nobody gets fired from a bank job unless they're caught stealing. Too many bankers seem to have a feeling that they can't fire anybody; it's almost like a social obligation to the community. We want our employees to feel secure in their bank job, but not so secure that they can do anything they want and get away with it. They're not working for the government. People take pride in their work when they know high standards are the norm. Every- body wants to be part of a winner. They don't want losers on their team. Other employees know who is pulling their weight and who is not. It bothers good employees more when underachievers are tolerated than when they're occa- sionally let go.

We should demand a lot, protect our people, reward out- standing work, and get rid of the nonperformers. It's hard to be proud of our bank if we know it has too many people not doing a first-rate job. We are not being fair to the good people when we force them to work with and depend upon incompetent coworkers or supervisors. It's never too late to start. We must bite the bullet, get it behind us, and get on with business.

We hate to dwell on the subject of firing people who are underperforming, but our experience tells us bankers do too little of it. We can invent programs and products and develop advertising and marketing campaigns, but if our tellers are grouchy, we've wasted our time and money. We must recognize that only our customer contact people can shape the public's perception of our bank. We can't successfully execute any kind of corporate strategy without their support and cooperation. We can build a great race car, but it won't perform on bad tires. Our reputation is established where the rubber meets the road.

Promote positive attitudes.   We must build positive attitudes throughout our bank. There should be no incessant complaining and endless dwelling on our own shortcomings. We must focus instead on all the things that we're doing to get better. We should promote optimism. It doesn't cost any more. Negative people produce negative results. Positive people produce positive results. Promote the positive thinkers. Do not reward the ability to perceive everything that is wrong with an idea. People who make a career out of identifying problems are not nearly as valuable as people who make a career out of constantly improving things so problems never get a chance to develop. We'll promote those with positive attitudes, they get things done.

We can start by eliminating all antagonistic relationships. There should be no "main office versus the branches" attitudes. We can't tolerate finger pointing between back room and frontline people. We must get them together and point them both in the same direction. People come to work each day wanting to do a good job. They should help each other do a good job. They shouldn't make problems for each other. We're all on the same team. When a football team wins a game, the whole team wins; and when they lose, the whole team loses. We'll make sure there are no bonus programs that allow one individual, department, division, or subsidiary to profit at the expense of another. We want to foster cooperation among our people, not competition. We'll compete with the bank across the street, not with each other. The boss and the employees are on the same side and both should believe that.

Support of bank policies. Everyone should be expected to support all bank policies. We don't all have to agree, but once the discussion is over and the decision has been made, then we should all pull in the same direction. We'll never blame the "main office" or the "loan committee" for anything. It doesn't help the bank's or the officers' image and reputation if the public sees bank officers disagreeing. If somebody on the inside thinks the bank is wrong, what is the customer to think? Besides, if the officer has trouble accepting what the bank is doing, why doesn't he leave? It doesn't speak well of the officer's integrity if he continues to accept pay from an employer that he disagrees with enough to tell the public about it. All officers and employees must be made to understand the difference between agreeing on all strategies and supporting them. We can never hope to get 100 people to agree on anything, but we can expect them to support the bank or leave, once the decisions are made.

We will never know if our strategies are good if they aren't supported by everybody. Those plans never have a chance to succeed. If we have a boat in which two people are rowing north and two are rowing south, we'll never find out which is right because the boat won't move in either direction.

The customer comes first. Everyone with lending authority should feel that he or she is on the customer's side. Although the loan officer represents the interests of the bank in all transactions, the loan officer is still on the customer's side because he or she should have the customer's best interests at heart.

When someone comes to our bank to arrange a loan, do we make him feel that he has done something wrong? "Well what have you done this time to require more help from your bank?" "When are you ever going to learn?" Does the borrower feel like he's going to confession? Or do our loan officers view the process as a mutually beneficial business transaction in which both parties help the other? Just a word, a phrase, or a look can create either atmosphere. The borrower can go out the door feeling important and wanted by his bank, or he can feel lousy, as if he had just been made to beg for something that should not have required him to be humbled or embarrassed. If we treat him poorly, no matter what the rate or terms on the loan, he won't be happy. We must look upon borrowers as the people who pay our salaries. We can't treat them like delinquent accounts before their first payment is due. We can't act like we're doing them a big favor, not even in the thousand little body language games people play.

When a borrower approaches a loan officer's desk, does the officer rise to greet the customer, smile broadly, call him by name, extend his hand for a warm, firm, and friendly handshake, and give the appearance of one who has rediscovered an old friend, or is the meeting a great deal less? When the customer approaches the loan officer, does the officer view him as an interruption in an otherwise peaceful day, or does the officer see the situation as an opportunity to shine? These things don't come naturally to many people. They have to be taught just as credit investigation, statement analysis, and credit evaluation must be taught. If we want our borrowers to come back over and over regardless of price, we must formally teach our loan officers how to treat people with exceptional courtesy and friendliness. It doesn't come naturally. They won't learn it at home.

All staff members are important. Everyone's job is important. We must make sure that all of the people who work for us treat all employees the way we'd like your children's employers to treat them. To consistently produce noticeably better service, everyone in the bank must perform well. They won't if they're not treated well by their superiors. If we dump on our branch managers, they'll dump on their tellers, and the tellers will dump on the customers. Our employees pass on what they receive and their bosses do the same. Respect for all employees must start at the top. People, no matter what their level, should never be reprimanded in public.

Let it be known in no uncertain terms that we positively will not tolerate sexual harassment or discrimination of any kind. We'll act quickly and decisively and won't make excuses for our officers if we find such behavior.

There are moral as well as economic reasons not to tolerate harassment or discrimination. Aside from the idea that we should do what our conscience tells us is the right thing, any lawsuit brought for a repeat offense by the same person will be many times more expensive because we ignored previous evidence of wrongdoing. If our conscience doesn't work, we can do it for the money.

Eliminate demotivators. People should have the equipment they need. Two tellers shouldn't have to share a $95.00 adding machine. They both need it at the same time. If the coffee machine is broken, replace it now. If people work overtime, pay them for every minute (it's the law). Don't pull rank. Even if people should do what the boss says simply because he is the boss, nobody should expect that type of response. It's better to have people question orders if they don't understand or if they think we may have overlooked something. People can save us, or they can perform silent sabotage by standing quietly by while we go down with the ship. We should help our employees become all they are capable of becoming. It should be a stated policy of our company to help our people grow. We'll never promote less competent people because we can't afford to lose the better person from his current job. We'll do everything we can to provide our employees with a positive work environment.

Promote integrity. Above all, we must demand and practice total and absolute integrity. If we return a check in error, first of all, we admit it without reservation. "We did it, and we're sorry." Don't say, "Well, if you hadn't used an unencoded deposit slip your deposit wouldn't have gone into the wrong account." If we accept unencoded deposit slips, we have an obligation to encode and process them correctly. We should refund any charges our bank made for the returned item, refund service charges that may have resulted from a lower average balance, refund any fees that the customer may have paid to the store where the check was returned, and write a letter to the store that clearly states the error was on the part of the bank. "We're sorry and we apologize for the inconvenience, and we want to be sure that this does not reflect adversely on the credit standing of our customer." Give the customer a copy of the letter; apologize again, and offer to pay for any out-of-pocket expenses that the customer may have incurred as a result of this error, such as phone calls, parking fees, or anything else that was ultimately the bank's fault. In the end, the customer will tell everyone about our great bank, and our employees will be proud to work for such an honest and considerate organization.

Besides the fact that practicing total honesty is the moral thing to do, there are very practical reasons for it as well.

We must be able to trust our officers and employees. If we allow them to practice less than total honesty with customers, we should realize they'll do the same with us. How can we effectively manage if we can't believe the people who are supplying us with critical information? How can we expect customers to be honest with our bank if our bank isn't honest in return? How can we maintain our reputation in the community if our integrity is in doubt? How can we expect the best people in the community to use our bank if they don't perceive our bank as a totally honorable organization? Why do dishonest people think nobody else knows it? Why do they think everybody else is dishonest?

We once had a lawyer who always said that we should never admit a mistake in writing because it could be used in court against us. That may or may not have been good legal advice, but it was bad common sense advice. If there is one thing that will drive a customer into a lawsuit, it is the blind stubborn unwillingness of the bank to admit it was wrong when indeed it was wrong. Any time a bank is involved in a lawsuit it has already lost. Legal services aren't free even if we win the case. The bank's reputation is hurt because many people assume the bank is wrong regardless of the merits of the case. If it gets before a jury, the bank has to prove its innocence beyond a reasonable doubt, and it still may be found guilty. The jury will believe the bank can afford the loss better than the individual. If the case is complicated, the bank has an even better chance of losing because very few jurors will fully understand what happened. When in doubt, blame the bank. We have seen a bank lose over one million dollars in the courtroom with a case that could have been settled by an apology in the very beginning.

Honesty is still the best policy. We should tell our people that no one should ever have to do anything on behalf of our bank that bothers their conscience. Nobody should lose a minute of sleep over anything that they do for the bank. It isn't necessary. We'll make more money by behaving honestly. If we have any questions about the ethics of anything we or our coworkers are doing, we should discuss it with our supervisors and put our minds at ease. If we are still troubled, bring it to the president and we'll get it resolved once and for all.

BUILDING A PROFESSIONAL IMAGE

It is very difficult to build a professional image for our bank without overtraining everybody. Unfortunately, many bank employees reach a point at a very early age when their formal training ends. Those employees will take two or three seminars and then decide it's just too much trouble. They then work for us for 40 more years and all they ever learn new about banking comes from another clerk who may or may not know what he's talking about.

A college graduate who went to work for IBM, was sent to a company-run school for 40 hours a week for nine weeks. That's the equivalent of giving our trainees about eight college courses in their first two months with us. What a difference in the competence of people if we did that and then insisted that they take two more courses each semester on their own time for the next several years.

Training

We should insist that all of our people take courses beyond the normal banking offerings. We have too many vice-presidents who can't spell, know very little grammar, and construct incomprehensible letters and memos. They'll tell us that it's the secretary's job to check the spelling. We usually tell them that we'd rather pay the secretary to write the letters. How do we know if our secretary can spell if we can't spell?

We should pay the full fee for a banking seminar and make it easier for our people to become more knowledgeable about banking. We should pay for other courses as well if they make our people more professional. We may have to limit the amount that we pay per course if we're near a university, or we'll be paying for MBAs for a lot of people who will then leave us. Even so, all employees should be encouraged to continually further their education.

In-house programs should be offered on those simple, easy, but rare qualities such as answering a telephone without irritating the person at the other end of the line. Anyone who has ever ordered a telephone from their local phone company knows it's possible to train young people to be pleasant and courteous on the phone and also to be pretty good salespeople. We always purchase more phone service than we thought we wanted.

Generally, we would say "yes" to seminars and "no" to conventions. A three-day drunk at company expense rarely does the bank any good, but two days at an investment seminar might give our investment officer one good idea that's worth a million dollars. We've had that happen.

There should be specific training that goes with every job. It could be a combination of in-house training, required reading, and certain banking courses at a local college, or courses offered by state or national banking organizations. Before someone becomes a branch manager, he/she should complete certain formal training, and after becoming a branch manager, there should be other courses and reading assignments that must be completed. After that, there should be on-going training of a more general nature. There can be three or four levels of branch managers each requiring more formal and informal training.

It's also important to cross-educate. Loan officers should know something about investments, the yield curve, the treasury markets, and pricing municipals and CDs. Then we might see better pricing in the loan area. We've actually seen banks offer loans at rates less than similar maturity governments. We can't for the life of us think of why, but it's embarrassing even though they don't work for our bank.

Every employee who has any type of customer contact needs training in the social graces. Several firms offer special courses for sales people or customer contact people, and they'll put together special programs for us at group rates. If we don't want to spend the money, we could send one training person and let that person build an in-house course for our own bank. We can't assume that sales skills come naturally.

Anyone who's been to Disney World knows that they run their parks by using a lot of young people who are obviously well-trained. We've been told that they train a new employee for two weeks before they'll let them take tickets at the gate, and it shows.

We can't expect our employees to cross-sell and present a professional appearance if they know nothing beyond their own jobs.

Dale Carnegie produces several training courses, as do other local concerns, that can help almost anyone gain self-confidence and improve interpersonal skills. It's an expensive undertaking, but it's very difficult to do a quality job in-house. Maybe we could hire a retired Dale Carnegie leader to run in-house programs. The problem here is that people on our payroll never carry the respect of an expert outsider.

If we are unhappy with any aspect of the service that we are providing, we can't just quietly accept it. Almost everything that is done in a bank has a well-produced training program to go with it. Some video training tapes available today are reasonably priced and much easier to use than the old 35mm movies.

Finally, unless we have a very small bank, training is too important to be part of the personnel or human resources department. We've never found human resources people to be any smarter or more pleasant than any other group in the bank. Good trainers need a teacher's background, a sincere interest in other people, a naturally pleasant personality, and lots of common sense. They also need some knowledge of what they are teaching. Most human resources people view training as a little piece of their responsibilities. It's much too important to be a part-time job. It's not something that we do only after all the required paperwork is caught up. The way our employees interact with our customers is more important than anything else they do. If we train them to treat customers the way that we want them to, we'll have a pretty good chance of success. If we don't train them, how can we expect them to come to the job knowing what is expected, and how to do it? We can't depend on our workers' parents to have instilled in them the attitudes and manners that we would like them to have.

Whatever else we do, we can't let untrained people answer the phone. It is amazing how some banks operate. Some banks hire a brand new teller, teach him how to accept deposits and cash checks, and just a few days later that same person is answering the telephone in a branch. As any branch manager knows, just about any question about banking that anybody can think of will eventually be directed toward a branch. Now we have a teller who has been with the bank two weeks answering the phone without having the slightest idea of the correct answer to 99% of the questions, or even a knowledge of where to go to get the answer. The initial response the customer receives can be so bad that the bank will never overcome it. If this seems like an exaggeration, we can test this by calling some of our branches at the number in the telephone book and asking for our bank's mortgage rates.

The bank's physical appearance. Everything in our bank, and especially our branches, should look new. When we buy a one-year-old used car, we get a vehicle that runs like a new one, but costs quite a but less than a new one. Even so, most people prefer a new car. Why? Because the new car has absolutely no dents, scratches, or rust marks. There are no spots on the carpet, and the windshield is absolutely clear. There is no dirt on heads of the dashboard buttons or in the creases of the upholstery, and the whole car just smells new. No matter how carefully we clean up a one-year-old car, we can't make it look new. Because of that, people are willing to pay a good deal more for a new car. Even though the one-year-old car runs like a new one, it doesn't look like a new one. Appearances are important.

When you take your car to be repaired at a Mercedes dealership, the man who fills out the forms in the service department wears a business suit. The mechanics wear white spotless coveralls. They all look new. These people are not grease monkeys. They may have been trained in Germany. The floor looks as if it's just been painted. We absolutely know this is going to be expensive, but they treat us like the owner's son, so we accept it. If price was our only concern, we wouldn't be there. We'd go to the corner garage where greasy rags are strewn all over, the floor is covered with dirt, and the mechanics look like they should be hosed down. We know it's not going to cost nearly as much at the corner garage. If they tried to charge us the same prices as the Mercedes garage, we'd be highly insulted. Yet the mechanic in the corner garage may be as good as or better than the mechanic in the Mercedes garage. He may be, but we don't think he is. Why not? How can we judge if we are not a mechanic? We can't. The Mercedes garage just looks more professional. The people who run it obviously care about appearances. Perhaps they also care about our car. They'll treat us politely, they won't get grease on our upholstery, they'll fix our car, and charge two and one-half times as much as the corner garage. We will pay it because they care, and if they must charge that much, they must hire only the best mechanics. Maybe true, maybe not, but appearances count.

Packaging is important. Anyone who has ever gone to the market to buy a box of cereal has at least once found a box on the floor, a little dirty but intact. Even though the box is dirty, we intellectually realize that inside the box, the cereal is protected in a wax paper bag. Although the box is dirty, the cereal is fine, so we take the dirty box, right? Wrong. We take a clean box. Why take a dirty one if a clean one is available at the same price?

Bank buildings are the same. If we've ever been in a new, recently opened branch building, we found everybody smiling. They are happy to be working in new surroundings. Their attitudes are infectious; even the customers feel it.

By contrast, if we go into a 75-year-old branch, one of those high ceiling dust bins, we might find way up at the top is a 50-watt bulb trying to make its light reach the floor. Everything is dark and nobody is smiling. The tellers simply can't get very excited in this work environment. Even an old building can be kept spotless, well-maintained, and especially well-lit, both inside and out. Brighter lights make people feel better.

Everything in the building must be spotless, especially the restrooms and lunchroom. Here, particularly, we're telling our employees what we think of them. If we don't show them that we're concerned about the little things, how can we expect them to be? We can't expect our employees to pay attention to detail if we don't lead by example.

We should routinely check everything. Does the furniture need refinishing or replacing? Is the carpeting worn? Is it soiled? Are the drapes clean? Do they match the rest of the decor? Do they need replacing? Does the parking lot need striping? Are there pot holes? Is there debris visible? Do the exterior signs need to be repainted? Are they easily read and understood? Is the landscaping being maintained or are the plants growing wild? Are the woodchips or pebbles strewn around the sidewalk? Is the grass cut? Or does the whole place look unkept? Every time someone from the main office visits a branch they should automatically check these things. The branch manager should be required to send in a checklist periodically, and somebody in the main office should be responsible for reacting.

We can't accept poor housekeeping. It sends a message to our customers that we don't care enough to pay attention to details. If the cleaning service isn't performing up to our standards, we must tell them about it until it's corrected. If we find it too much bother to continually remind them, replace them. If all else fails, we can hire our own cleaning people and insist on getting what we want. Many topflight department stores do this routinely. So do many expensive restaurants. How do they do it? They set high standards. They don't accept what the cleaning service offers, so they hire their own people. A good work environment sets the tone. Nobody works well in a messy, poorly maintained building.

When a customer enters a Nordstrom's department store for the first time, he or she just knows the merchandise will cost more than at Kmart's. We don't have to check the prices, we expect to pay more. The surroundings are better and so is the service. One chain competes on the basis of price, and the other does not. There's nothing wrong with competing on price elsewhere, but it's almost impossible in banking.

When customers walk into one of our branches, do they think of Kmart of Nordstrom? If they think Kmart, we can't charge like Nordstrom. Our buildings should show a pride of ownership. In any neighborhood there's usually at least one house that stands out from the rest, not as the biggest but as the obviously best maintained. We immediately know the owner cares. Our bank building also sends a message.

Finally, we should set a schedule and completely refurbish every branch every five or six years. We could do 15% or 20% of our branches every year. We shouldn't just replace the carpeting when it becomes tattered, then replace the drapes later, and the wallpaper later still. If we do the whole thing at once it can all be coordinated. We'll refinish or repaint the furniture at the same time. Our employees will love it, and so will our customers. We'll project the image of an up-to-date organization that cares about its employees and depositors. We'll create excitement in our staff a whole year before they are due for remodeling. It doesn't cost any more in the long run to do it all at once, but the effect is much more striking. Obviously, we'll do the worst offices first and the newest last. Above all, we'll brighten up everything. People work better in a "like-new" environment and our reputation is enhanced in the eyes of our customers.

Faster service. We should do everything faster. We can no longer "sleep" on decisions. While we are "sleeping on it," someone else is taking care of our customer. Society today wants and expects everything instantly. We don't have to like it, but we better be ready to deliver it. If we don't, our competitor will and we'll be left behind.

More specifically, we should return phone calls faster. When we get back to our desk, do we return calls in minutes, hours, or days? If somebody calls us right now, it's because they want to speak to us right now, not three hours from now and not tomorrow. When someone calls, is the phone answered on the first ring or does it ring eight or 10 times before someone picks it up? What kind of image does that project? If we can't answer the phone professionally, how on earth can we handle a residential mortgage that is much more complex? Many customers can receive a negative impression of our bank before they ever talk to us.

Cash checks faster. How can we do that, knowing full well that we can't afford to staff our branches to handle the busiest times of the week? Well, there are some things that we can do. They are very simple things that very often are not done.

It seems obvious, but we can make sure everyone is working at the busiest time of the day. One bank president once walked into a small village three teller branch. At high noon they had one teller working and a line at least 20 people deep. The manager was sitting at his desk reading a newspaper. The president asked the manager where all the tellers were. He looked around as if noticing for the first time that there was a line out to the door. "Helen must be in the back running checks." He was told to get her out on the window to get the line down. The manager said the courier would be by soon to pick up the work. The president told him the customers were more important than the courier. The manager said the people in the data center might be upset. The president told him he was getting a lot more upset. The manager got the teller out of the back room and now he had two lines 10 deep.

The president asked where the third teller was. "Florence is at lunch." When asked why he let her go to lunch at high noon on a Friday, he said, "Florence has been going to lunch at noon for 17 years." The president said, "Well you explain to Florence that if I can do without her during the busiest time of the day, I can do without her the rest of the day!"

There are two things that really bother customers when they wait in line. It really irritates them when they get into a line that doesn't move. Somebody in front of them has the company payroll or the town's deposits. They wait and wait, move to another line, and then that one stops. Our customers should not have to tolerate this. Most branches today arrange ropes so the customer can go to the next available teller and never get stuck in a line that's not moving. People don't mind lines that move.

Another thing that drives customers crazy is having someone behind the counter who is not waiting on customers. They don't mind waiting if they happen to get to the bank at a busy time and everybody is doing their best to take care of things. But if one or two people are running checks or opening night bags, they are making customers wait longer than necessary. If we have customers in line, we should take care of them first and do the other work later. If we absolutely must do those other things instead of take care of customers, it should be done in the back room, the lunch room, or even the boiler room. Customers will be patient if we're doing all that we can do to take care of them, but they get very impatient if we make them wait while we do something else. We shouldn't blame them because we'd feel the same way.

Finally, a good teller can overcome the irritation of a long wait by doing a good job when the customer finally gets to the window. Does our teller smile, call the customer by name, and say, "I'm sorry you had to wait so long, sometimes everybody seems to show up at the same time." And then when the transaction is over, does our teller hand the receipt to the customer instead of throwing it on the counter? The teller should conclude the transaction with "Have a nice weekend," or "See you next week," or "Thanks for coming in." With proper handling, a teller can send a customer out the door feeling important and appreciated. Happy customers forget the wait and remember the service.

Our tellers won't do these things if we don't train them to. If our teller training focuses entirely on preventing loss, our tellers will treat each customer like a potential thief. It's what we've taught them to do.

We should all correct errors faster. We can't be content to phone the information to operations and then wait three or four days for an answer. Follow up! That customer is upset with our bank until the problem is resolved. The longer it takes us to fix it, the more upset the customer becomes. It doesn't matter whose fault it turns out to be. If our customer is upset with us for two or three days, it doesn't disappear when we explain that it was the customer's fault. We'd almost rather it was our fault. Then the customer can say, "I told you so," and forget it. When it turns out to be the customer's error, it's as if we've added insult to injury. Not only was the customer upset for three days, we've denied him his ultimate victory.

We must never forget there are no minor problems. It may be routine for us, but it is not routine for the customer.

Approve loans faster. On most consumer loan requests the credit investigation can be completed in about 15 minutes. When it's done, we should make a decision and immediately communicate it to the customer. We can send a man to the moon, perform a couple dozen experiments, and bring him back to Earth in less time than it takes most banks to approve a mortgage. Bankers have allowed themselves to become trapped by the demands of the secondary markets. In the years ahead if we can't approve a mortgage in a day with a satisfactory appraisal being the only contingency, then we just won't be able to compete. We're going to have to do it sooner or later just to stay even. Why not start now and get a jump on our competitors?

Although I live in Albany, New York, I sometimes must travel to the West Coast. My wife had never had a charge card at Nordstrom because there wasn't a Nordstrom store within 500 miles of our home.

Once I went into a Nordstrom in Portland, Oregon to buy a few things to bring back to Albany. I chose a sweater for my wife, and the sales girl smiled and said, "Sir, will that be cash or would you like to put it on your Nordstrom charge card?" I told her, I would pay cash. "Do you have a Nordstrom charge card?" I said no, I didn't. "Would you like a Nordstrom charge card? It will only take a minute." I said, "No thank you."

As I went upstairs to get something for a daughter, I thought it might be fun to get a card for my wife. She loved Nordstrom and always shopped there when she was with me. I decided to accept the card offer if I were asked again.

Upstairs I went through exactly the same routine. "Sir, will that be cash or would you like to put it on your Nordstrom charge card? Do you have a Nordstrom charge card? Would you like a Nordstrom charge card?" I told her that I lived 3,000 miles away, but that I'd like one if I could get one. She pulled out a very short application and asked me my name and address, employer, social security number, driver's license number, and major credit card number. The whole process took less than a minute. She picked up the phone, repeated the information, and asked me if I'd like the sweater gift wrapped. I said no, I'd be flying back and it would just get squashed in my luggage. She said, "Well, would you like a flattened box that you could put together back home?" "No thank you," I said. She then hung up the phone and told me, "Mr. Brown, it will take about two weeks to get your card prepared, but your credit is approved, and I can put this purchase on your new account if you'd like." The imprinted card arrived in Albany, New York, four days later. We've got to love a company like that.

We should make hustle part of our image. Become known as a bank that gets things done fast. If we move fast, we look like we're working hard; we show our customers we really care about service. Banks with a reputation for being hard to deal with are very often just plain slow. It doesn't work anymore.

GETTING YOUR BANK TO TREAT CUSTOMERS RIGHT

How do we get everybody in the bank to treat every customer like the president's spouse? First, we check up on everything. We have our secretary call a few branches and ask about car loans and tape the answers. Then play the tapes at our next officers meeting. We'll offer constructive criticism. All of the calls won't be terrible. We'll compliment the good ones. Once people know that we'll be checking, there will be widespread immediate improvement. They will be more careful.

We could send a short form questionnaire to every new account asking how the customer was treated. Were they offered a savings account, a charge card, a safe deposit box? Did our people explain everything to their satisfaction? Does the customer have any unanswered questions? Does the customer have any comments on how we could improve? Anytime that any employee is mentioned by name, good or bad, he or she gets a copy of the response. If the letters come straight to the president's office and are not prescreened, it is not necessary for the president to personally read every single letter. Just knowing that he reviews some of them straight out of the envelope will produce immediate results. We should then make a fuss about the good ones. We'll give awards such as teller of the month, branch of the month, and manager of the month. The best of the year gets to take his or her family to Disneyland for a week.

We could pay employees a few dollars for every positive comment. We won't have to say a word about the bad ones, although we sometimes will feel compelled to take action.

When we first start this program, it will be a real eye-opener. We will never forget the morning the first letter began, "Dear Mr. Brown, How brave of you to solicit my comments." The woman had good reason to complain, we were able to cure the problem immediately and turned a very bad situation into a very good one. The branch manager who took the application assured the woman that the rate and points he quoted her on her mortgage application would not change. At the time, we did not establish rates at application, but at commitment. She received a commitment letter for a higher rate. Because of time constraints she went ahead with the transaction, closed the loan, fumed about the injustice for over a month, told all of her friends about it; and when our routine customer survey arrived, decided to send us a three-page letter. Upon investigation, we were convinced that it happened just as she said. Unfortunately, we couldn't unclose a mortgage, especially after it had been sold into the secondary market. We mathematically calculated that if we refunded $930 in "points," the effect would be to produce the same annual percentage rate as she had been promised. We wrote her a letter, apologized, explained our calculation, enclosed a check for $930, and told her to call if she didn't consider this remedy to be satisfactory. She wrote another letter about a month later expressing total astonishment that a bank would do that, brought all of her accounts back to us, and showed our letter to everyone she knew. Most banks probably would try to avoid that expensive an adjustment. We did it for two reasons. First, for that money, we couldn't buy that amount of good word-of-mouth publicity; and more importantly, it was the right thing to do. People appreciate it when the president takes a personal interest in their well-being.

If we train our people in customer courtesy, there will be a difference; if we don't, there won't. These things are simple, but they're not easy and they're not common sense. When our bank is known as the friendliest and most caring financial institution in our marketplace, we will be able to pay one-quarter percent less, charge one-quarter percent more, and keep our customer base. When we do that, earnings will not be our most pressing problem.

As we've said before, in banking, little things mean a lot. Although the differences between the best and worst performing banks are small, they are extremely important to success. We're not talking about overcharging customers by an exorbitant amount. We're talking about delivering a product that is noticeably better and charging a little more for it.

Every officer and employee in the bank should understand that their primary objective is to increase our shareholder's value. We do that with high earnings. Providing outstanding service is a method to help us achieve our objective. It is not our objective. We want to give superior service at a modest cost so we can improve earnings. The customer must believe that he is getting more than his money's worth. Our employees must understand the difference between the means and the end. This is not widely understood, but it is critically important.

If our employees believe that our primary objective is to produce "customer satisfaction" or to "serve the community," then they won't understand or support our strategies. If our primary objective was to make our customer happy, we'd charge lower rates on loans, pay higher rates on deposits, reduce or eliminate service charges and fees, reduce our credit standards, and overstaff our branches so that nobody would ever have to wait. Our employees can logically conclude that those are all things that we should do if we want happy customers. How can they support our programs if they perceive them to be irrational? They must be taught the difference between the means and the end. The end is higher earnings, and one of the means to that end is great customer service. We are supplying great customer service so that our customers will be willing to pay a little more for our products. Since we can't make it up in volume, our only alternative is to make more money with what we have, and to do that we need superior service. When every officer and employee is doing all they can to treat customers like royalty, margins can improve and superior earnings will follow. If all of our employees don't have any idea of what we are trying to accomplish, and how it will work, they will defeat our best plans in a thousand small ways without even knowing that they are doing it.

All of our employees must understand that we are trying to improve earnings by achieving customer satisfaction. We are trying to achieve customer satisfaction by providing desirable features other than price. We want to supply superior value. Our employees must also understand how their performance fits into this big picture. They must understand exactly what they must do to uphold their piece of our overall plan.

They can't figure this out for themselves. It must be explained clearly by the most senior member of management available. We can list thousands of ways to improve customer service, but our employees will not embrace any of them if, in their perception, senior management is not doing some of the simple things that are within their power to improve customer service. "If senior management won't raise deposit rates, why do they expect me to cross-sell?" Only when our employees understand our goals and strategies, and can tell one from the other, will they do all in their power to make them work.

Finally, we must try to look ahead to determine what will constitute satisfactory service in the future, and do it now. If we provide those changes first we can gain an edge on our competition. We probably shouldn't waste time trying to invent unique new products. New products are too hard to sell because few people understand what they are.

Within a few years most banks will approve consumer loans in less than an hour. Some are doing it now. We could gear up for it and be the first in our marketplace. It will help establish our image as a hustling company that puts the customer first. We could approve mortgages in a day; correct errors in a day; or establish a 24-hour consumer loan hotline.

We should probably greatly expand our banking hours. Is there any other retail business that closes at 3:00 p.m.? Imagine your local supermarket advertising, "If you want food, you have to get here by 3:00 p.m.!" Banking hours have to expand. Banks should be open at least 40 to 60 hours a week. We can gain a competitive edge if we are the first to introduce expanded hours—or lose market share if we are the last.

Superior customer service is not complicated, but it is not easy. Those companies with a high service reputation are the ones willing to work hard to improve in a thousand little ways and take time to follow up to be sure they are delivering the level of quality intended.

SUMMARY

Too many bankers take good service for granted. Bankers themselves generally receive good service from their own banks so they don't perceive a need for improvement. They also find it difficult to make any firm connections between good service and increased earnings. In fact, most bankers believe that it costs more to provide better service.

Even so, bankers must recognize that if they compete on the basis of price, simple arithmetic prevents them from outperforming their peers. If they can't win by competing on price, they must come to understand that high quality service is the only other way to attract customers, and if they can learn to offer service that is really better than their competitors, they can be successful. The hardest part is learning, perhaps through experience, that better service does not have to cost more.

10 ACTION PLAN

It's now time to use everything we've examined here and build an action plan designed to improve our current level of earnings. We'll start by setting certain internally consistent goals. These should include desired capital ratio, dividend payout ratio, earnings per share growth, return on assets, and return on equity. We can add others if we want, but we should be careful not to muddy the waters. No goals are set in stone. They are simply steps along the way. When the goals are approached or achieved, we don't all go to sleep; we figure out how to do a little better and set new goals. The long-range goal should be to improve earnings per share every year by an amount that is at least 2% or 3% above the inflation rate.

As mentioned earlier, we begin by choosing a peer group that we want to be part of. Deciding which banks should be included is critical. They should all be of the same general size. If we have a 100-million-dollar bank, the size range should be from $75 to $400 million. We shouldn't compare our bank to multibillion-dollar banks. They are different in too many ways.

We also want banks from similar markets. If our bank is located in western Massachusetts, we shouldn't compare ourselves to a bank in Boston. Something in Vermont, New Hampshire, and northern Connecticut would be better. Even the Middle Atlantic States or upstate New York would provide more similar market characteristics. If possible, it's always better to confine our peer group to banks in our home state. Then we're all operating under the same laws, rules, and regulations. On the other hand, we shouldn't get too picky in trying to choose our peer group. No two markets are identical, and they don't have to be for our purposes.

We should make sure that our peer group generally outperforms our bank. We want to learn how to get better, not worse. We can't hope to improve by studying a group of banks that don't do as well as we do. This whole exercise is designed to produce better earnings for our bank. If, however, we expect to share peer group data with our board of directors on a regular basis, then prudence would dictate the inclusion of at least two or three banks that we outperform. Ideally, our bank should be compared with other banks in our state to see how we're doing, and that data can be shared with the board and our shareholders. But for purposes of developing a strategic plan, we need to study the high performers, and perhaps this process should be kept confidential. There is a psychological factor involved that can't be overlooked. If all the data the board ever sees is negative, after a while they will believe that they have a very poor bank. It can affect our self-image, the board's opinion of management, and management's collective morale, not to mention its longevity.

After we have chosen a group of eight or ten good performers, we'll obtain their most recent annual reports. We can simply ask to be put on a mailing list for their reports and offer to exchange our own. If we have a holding company, we can buy a few hundred shares of their stock and we'll routinely receive everything they put out. We must be careful not to buy the stock ourselves if there is any chance that we may ever buy their bank. The SEC might have us put in jail if our purchase constitutes insider trading. When we finally have all of the peer group's annual reports, we'll spread their balance sheets together with our own. We'll do the same with their income statements. Alongside of each item on their (and our) income statements, we'll place a percent. We'll measure each item as a percentage of "average total assets."

We'll summarize the following five critical numbers as a percentage of average total assets: total interest income, total interest expense, loan loss provision, noninterest income, and total overhead. These should lead us to before tax income. It is important to calculate these ratios as a percentage of average total assets. It's the only way to accurately measure one bank against another. Some accountants like to start with total interest income, making that equal to 100%, and then calculate all other items of interest and expense as a percentage of that number. We really don't like that approach. We won't be able to tell if our overhead is too high or our interest income is too low. We want to be able to measure each of the five elements independently so that we'll know exactly where we stand with each. Any measurement or ratio that uses two or more of the five parts of the income statement lends itself to confusion. Some analysts like to measure overhead as a percentage of noninterest income. If the result is unsatisfactory, we're not sure which of the numbers is off. It's pointless to work on the wrong problem.

Quickly review Table 10.1. Here we have the income statements of nine banks arrayed as a percentage of total assets. Most are pretty good earners. Bank E has the highest yielding assets and Bank B has the lowest. Presenting the figures this way still doesn't quite show us what we want.

Table 10.1 Income and Expense Categories Presented as a Percent of Average Total Assets

Peer Group Income Analysis	Bank A	Bank B	Bank C	Bank D	Bank E	Bank F	Bank G	Bank H	Bank I	Peer Group Average
Interest Income	9.53%	8.97%	9.71%	9.84%	9.85%	9.65%	9.34%	8.98%	9.45%	9.48%
Interest Expense	4.92	4.50	5.21	4.42	5.02	4.23	4.62	5.04	5.15	4.79
Interest Margin	4.61	4.47	4.50	5.42	4.83	5.42	4.72	3.94	4.30	4.69
Less: Loan Loss Provision	0.43	0.30	0.31	0.27	0.26	0.32	0.13	0.02	0.51	0.28
Plus: Other Income	0.72	0.82	0.56	0.85	1.17	0.99	1.25	0.81	1.05	0.91
Less: Overhead	3.05	3.11	3.09	3.68	3.98	4.35	4.67	3.60	3.54	3.67
Pretax Income	1.85	1.89	1.66	2.32	1.76	1.73	1.18	1.13	1.30	1.65

We should now take the group average of each of these percents and determine in which areas we are above average and below average. We can quickly determine whether our bank outperforms or underperforms the peer group in interest income, interest expense, loan loss provision, non-interest income, and overhead. This isolates our strong and weak points so that we can determine where to concentrate our efforts. We can and probably should try to improve all of these ratios, but if we already have the lowest overhead to total assets ratio, there would seem to be better opportunities to improve earnings in other parts of the bank. The whole purpose of this exercise is to focus attention on those areas in our bank that would present the best opportunities for earnings improvement.

Review Table 10.2. This shows how many basis points each peer group bank is over or under the group average. On this table we tried not to create confusion caused by trying to figure out whether a negative variance on expense items is good or bad. Any negative variances hurt earnings. All minuses are bad.

After we have determined how many basis points our bank is above or below the peer group average, we multiply that difference by our average total assets, and we'll be able to see how many dollars our bank is making or losing by being over or under the high performing peer group average in each of the five major categories.

Table 10.3 converts those basis points into dollars for each peer group bank. We can see that Bank A does better than average with interest income and does extremely well on overhead. However it pays $3.1 million more in interest expense, $3.4 million more in loan loss provision, and receives $4.5 million less in noninterest income than it would if it equalled the peer group average. Bank B, on the other hand, suffers primarily in the interest income category. These two banks should be developing earnings improvement

Table 10.2 Each Bank's Variance from the Peer Group Average

Variance from Peer Group Average	Bank A	Bank B	Bank C	Bank D	Bank E	Bank F	Bank G	Bank H	Bank I
Interest Income	0.05%	-0.51%	0.23%	0.35%	0.37%	0.17%	-0.14%	-0.50%	-0.03%
Interest Expense	-0.13	0.29	-0.42	0.37	-0.23	0.56	0.17	-0.25	-0.36
Interest Margin	-0.08	-0.22	-0.19	0.73	0.14	0.73	0.03	-0.75	-0.39
Less: Loan Loss Provision	-0.15	-0.02	-0.03	0.01	0.02	-0.04	0.15	0.26	-0.23
Plus: Other Income	-0.19	-0.09	-0.35	-0.06	0.26	0.08	0.34	-0.10	0.14
Less: Overhead	0.62	0.56	0.58	-0.01	-0.31	-0.68	-1.00	0.07	0.13
Pretax Income	0.20	0.24	0.01	0.67	0.11	0.08	-0.47	-0.52	-0.35

Note: Each negative variance reduces net income.

Table 10.3 Dollar Impact on Earnings of Each Variance (000s)

Variance from Peer Group Average Actual Dollars (000)	Bank A	Bank B	Bank C	Bank D	Bank E	Bank F	Bank G	Bank H	Bank I
Interest Income	1,199	-10,558	3,680	3,590	3,665	1,589	-1,156	-3,968	-217
Interest Expense	-3,050	6,016	-6,688	3,783	-2,272	5,199	1,415	-1,988	-2,700
Interest Margin	-1,851	-4,541	-3,008	7,373	1,394	6,787	259	-5,956	-2,917
Less: Loan Loss Provision	-3,441	-346	-425	136	230	-340	1,276	2,094	-1,700
Plus: Other Income	-4,535	-1,936	-5,626	-648	2,535	712	2,808	-822	1,025
Less: Overhead	14,649	11,710	9,306	-57	-3,018	-6,271	-8,285	592	1,008
Pretax Income	4,882	4,887	248	6,805	1,141	887	-3,948	-4,092	-2,583

Note: Each negative variance reduces net income

plans that focus in entirely different areas. They both do well with overhead control, but there the similarity ends.

Bank G obviously has an overhead problem, as do banks D, E, and F. Bank H needs help in every area but loan quality.

It seems clear that any plan to improve earnings must take into account the particular strengths and weaknesses of the individual bank. A single approach doesn't work equally well in all banks. One size doesn't fit all.

Almost always, one or two categories will present us with large potentials for improvement. We should focus our energies on those areas. Eventually, we will want our bank to be above average in each category, but in the beginning, we'll concentrate on those areas with the greatest potential rewards.

If our overhead is too high, we'll check further among our peers to see if it's from salaries and benefits, occupancy, or other expenses. Although it is usually salaries, we may discover "other expenses" are out of line, and this will help to further zero in on the items that need attention. If interest expense is too high, we'll compare the rate breakdowns available to see if anything in particular suggests itself. We'll get as much information as possible from the peer group comparison on those categories that we decide to attack. We'll then reread those pertinent chapters in this book.

Finally, we'll put together the elements of our plan as it will apply in our bank. We'll lay out exactly what we want to accomplish, who will do it, when they will do it, when they will report back and to whom, and how frequently we and our management group will meet to monitor progress. This would normally be a multifaceted attack. We generally can't solve complex bank problems by pushing a single button.

We can't expect instant success, but we should just make sure that whatever movement is discernible is in the right direction. However, before this plan can be implemented, it must be communicated to every officer in the bank, even those who may not be directly involved. We should bring together all officers in the bank and show them slides or overheads, beginning with some of the tables in this book. We'd explain the idea of the peer group and show them how we compare with our peers.

We'll produce tables showing how our bank compares with each of our peers in each of the five categories. We'll show our officers how much more our bank would earn if we produced at the group average—not at the level of the best in the group, at the average.

We'd then explain step-by-step just what we want everybody to do in order to produce the desired results. The program starts with the premise that we will never again compete on the basis of price. No matter how much time we spend explaining all the steps that we will take to improve interest income or reduce overhead, the program must end with an in-depth explanation of all the things everybody must try to do in order to make our bank worthy of the prices that we will charge. A lot of time must be spent communicating to build a friendly, professional group of bankers who sincerely want to help their customers. After the officers understand all facets of the plan, they must communicate the information to every employee in the bank.

We should ask for and obtain the support of every officer in the bank. Every officer with a loan limit will have to sell a little harder to obtain better rates, and if they do, the results will be immediate and eye opening.

If we have a loan quality problem, we are in for a much longer effort. It takes about three years to turn over a loan portfolio and really clean it out. The immediate need is to be sure that we can stop the bleeding. We'll immediately do all that is necessary to stop adding fuel to the fire. This may be the most difficult kind of problem to solve.

Once everyone knows exactly what is expected, we must follow up with critical measurements to determine that we are indeed moving in the right direction. We'll hold follow-up meetings every three to six months so that everybody is aware of and feels a part of the progress. We'd ask for input from everybody on ways to accomplish our goals. Tellers know what they can do to improve service if management will agree with their ideas. Just getting them together to talk about better service, and asking for their input, will improve the level of service. We will also be surprised to learn how some of them are really smart and discerning. We should recognize outstanding performance.

As our bank moves along in the right direction, we'll advance our goals. In the beginning it's fine to try to meet the high performing peer group average, but as we get better, we will want to move to the head of the line in at least some categories. It's nice to be best at something. Before we get to the point where we are outperforming our peer group, we should build a new, even better performing peer group. Periodically we'll eliminate a poor performer and replace it with a high performer. Over time we can expect some of our peers to be bought or to fall by the wayside. We'll replace them with better performers. Eventually we will find our bank running with the thoroughbreds.

All of the things that we've discussed in this book are represented by fairly simple ideas and concepts. They're easy to understand, but they're not easy to do. Many managers would like to believe that the road to success is paved with complex ideas and procedures that their competition can't duplicate. This simply isn't so. The idea of providing service that is so outstanding that people will pay more for it is not hard to understand. Federal Express charges about one hundred times what the post office charges, but thousands of people pay that price every day. Superior service in a bank is very difficult to deliver; and because it's so hard to deliver, most of us would prefer to find an easy "secret formula" for success. It doesn't exist.

Above all, we must have patience. Banks are a lot like battleships; it takes a while to get them to change direction. We just have to make sure that we are moving steadily closer to our goals at a pace that is acceptable to our board and our stockholders.

Once we are ahead of the peer group average in every category, we may reach the point where we are competing with ourselves. By continually trying to review and improve service and productivity, we will find our bank achieving new heights of performance, and we'll discover that we have a group of officers and employees who are eager to come to work everyday. They will be proud to tell new acquaintances where they work. They will smile a lot because we will be appropriately rewarding them for this outstanding performance. Finally, our board of directors will want to reward us with stock options, new perks, and golden parachutes. Unfortunately, our own board and family are usually the last people to recognize how great a job we are doing. They're too close to us and may concentrate too much on our weak points. Other bankers, however, know the difference between average performance and super performance. And we know, which is the most important thing of all.

We have followed the strategies outlined in this book for a number of years, and they have always worked well. They do not represent the only way to manage a high performing bank, but they have worked in many very different banks. They are working right now in banks like yours that are being run by people like you. Developing and using this approach to high quality banking has consistently produced above average results. It is something that requires determination by all involved. That determination must start at the top and spread throughout the organization. We can help with the plan and the process, but you must supply the determination, the perseverance, and the follow-up to produce a consistently high performing bank.

INDEX

About the Author

Albert J. Brown, Jr. is president of The Belvedere Group, Inc., Albany, New York, a bank consulting firm specializing in earnings improvement workshops. Unlike most consultants, Mr. Brown helps bankers help themselves by laying out a road map to greater earnings.

Before striking out on his own, Mr. Brown had over 33 years experience in commercial banking, all of it within the KeyCorp organization. As president and CEO of a commercial bank, he improved the return on assets from .50 to 1.03 in three years. In addition, he formed his company's residential mortgage company where over five years as chairman and president, he produced an average return on equity of approximately 20%. He also assisted in the formation of a nationwide mail-deposit bank and served as its chairman. In less than five years, this bank grew to over $500 million in assets and produced a return on assets in excess of 1.00%.

Mr. Brown has been executive vice president of KeyCorp where he has served in a variety of capacities. He has been chairman of the holding company's asset liability committee, he has worked in mergers and acquisitions, served on the loan policy committee, been in charge of the corporation's mortgage companies, been responsible for management of other real estate nationwide, and has provided investment advice to subsidiary banks.

Mr. Brown has served on the boards of Key Bancshares of New York, Key Bank of Southeastern New York NA, Key Bank USA NA, Key Bank of Northern New York NA, Key Life Insurance, Key Venture Capital, Key Mortgage Funding, Key Pacific Mortgage Company, All Coast Financial Inc., Key Mortgage Services, Key Services Company, and NCB Properties, all of which are or were KeyCorp subsidiaries.

Down through the years, Mr. Brown has been active in many community organizations. He has been chairman of the board of Child Find of America, a nonprofit organization that locates kidnapped children, and of Maria College in Albany. He has produced two child safety videos for Child Find.

Mr. Brown graduated from Manhattan College and the Stonier Graduate School of Banking. He is the author of *The Effective Branch Manager*, another publication of Probus Publishing Company.

Mr. Brown has nine children. He and his wife, the former Susan E. Gladding, live in Menands, New York, a suburb of Albany.